The Light of the Heart

The Light of the Heart

An Introduction to
the Principles and
Practices of Sufism

❦

As taught by Sufi Masters
Seyedeh Nahid Angha, Ph.D. and
Shah Nazar Seyed Ali Kianfar, Ph.D.

Halima JoAnn Haymaker

**International Association
Of Sufism Publications**

Copyright © 2017 Halima JoAnn Haymaker
ISBN-13: 9780986359262
ISBN-10: 0986359262
Library of Congress Control Number: 2017938375
International Association of Sufism

This book does not imply any gender bias by the use of feminine or masculine terms, nouns or pronouns.

The International Association of Sufism is a publisher of many Sufi books and Sufi related materials. Books published by the IAS are the authors' views and the publisher takes no responsibility for any statement made by the authors in its publications.

For more information address the publisher:

International Association of Sufism
P.O. Box 2382
San Rafael, CA 94912
USA

Cover Design by Matthew Davis, Ph.D.

Do you know me, oh dear heart?
I am but life from the Beloved,
Not just mere clay but rather
The light of the heart
Breathed into the heart of dust.

Moulana Shah Maghsoud Sadegh Angha
From *Ecstasy: The World of Sufi*
Poetry and Prayer
By Nahid Angha

The meaning of the Qur'an is discovered by the Light of the Heart.

Shah Nazar Seyed Ali Kianfar

All Praise to Allah
The One and Only

Gratitude to the
Holy Master of Our Tariqat
Hazrat Pir Moulana Shah Maghsoud Sadegh
Angha

All Thanks Always to
Beloved Wise Teachers
Seyedeh Nahid Angha
And
Shah Nazar Seyed Ali Kianfar

Dedication

With gratitude and love to my husband,
Will Haymaker;
to my sons, Barton Willian Edson and
John Hank Hamid Edson;
and to my grandson, Colton Rae Edson.
All have given me inspiration,
support and love

Introduction

On March 30, 1996, Allah granted me one of the greatest blessings of my life when my son, John Hank Hamid Edson, introduced me to his Sufi Masters, Seyedeh Nahid Angha and Shah Nazar Seyed Ali Kianfar. For more than a year and a half I met with them, in addition to attending two international Sufism symposia as their guest, before I realized God had sent me to them. With all praise to the One, they accepted me as their student and welcomed me into the Uwaiysi tariqat. During the past 20 years they have taught me and surrounded me with their loving care, even when I have been slow to learn. In 2002 my beloved teachers gave me the Sufi name Halima, the name of the nurse of the Prophet Mohammad, peace be upon him. I was later given the title of Sheikha, and on

August 30, 2014, I received the great honor of being appointed to teach Uwaiysi Sufism.

In writing this book I attempt to distill into simple form the teachings I have received over the past 20 years along with some added commentary from scholars whose work has provided me with information. May these words serve as an introduction to Sufism for those who long to know.

By using the feminine pronoun throughout, I attempt to balance the use of the masculine pronoun during the past many centuries.

All unattributed information and all wisdom in this book come from the oral teachings of my holy teachers, Dr. Nahid Angha and Dr. Ali Kianfar. I offer them my deepest gratitude. I am also indebted to their teacher Hazrat Pir Moulana Shah Maghsoud Sadegh Angha, 20th century Persian Sufi Master. All quotations from the Holy Qur'an are from the 1987 version by Abdullah Yusuf Ali.[1]

Any errors of fact and interpretation in this book are my own, and for them I apologize.

Table of Contents

CHAPTER 1

What Is Sufism?

❧

- *Why is the Sufi poet Rumi the most widely read poet in America?*
- *What keeps the Sufi whirling dervishes standing up in their ecstatic turning?*
- *Why is Sufism sometimes secret and sometimes banned in certain countries?*
- *Why are Sufis often called "the drunken ones" when, as Muslims, they abstain from drinking alcohol?*
- *Why is Sufism sometimes called the journey of lovers?*

What is this thing called Sufism?
This ancient practice is followed
by more than
65 million people around the
world today.

SUFISM IS A PATH--THE MYSTICAL path of Islam, the path of inner searching. This is a way of exploration for those who want to know: know themselves, where they came from, where they are going--and want to know God. It is a journey to find the hidden self.

"Mysticism" is a word that is often not clearly understood. It means "experiential knowledge of spiritual things," as opposed to information obtained from reading, sermons or lectures.[1]

The basic principle of Sufism is the rule of unity: *There is nothing except the Divine, the source of all being;* or "there is nothing but an ultimate Unity." [2] To understand this is to know all beings are part of the Divine, just as separate drops of water are part of the great ocean. Through meditation the Sufi experiences herself as part of the oneness of all creation. The Sufi journey to God culminates when she enters "the oceans of divine knowledge."[3]

The practice of Sufism is the search for knowledge. This knowledge is found through the experience of coming to know oneself through an inner journey to an unseen world, through meditation. The goal of the Sufi is to *experience* the presence of God, the Beloved, the Divine, within the self. There is a saying of the Prophet Mohammad (peace be upon him), "Whoever knows oneself, knows one's Lord."

The Sufi's quest is to return to her pure inner self, the self that came with her when she came from God and was born into this physical body. To know this pure inner self is to experience oneness with the divine essence of all being. Sufism may be described as "a remembrance of the Supreme Self which infinitely transcends the human ego."[4]

According to Sufi Master Dr. Ali Kianfar, "Sufism is a spiritual system that enables seekers to take the inner path to self-awareness directly through and for themselves, in order to arrive at the source of tranquility."[5]

Sufis believe the logic of the physical mind cannot comprehend the infinite God and God cannot be described in human language. Instead, only through meditation and opening the heart can an individual come to have a direct experience of Truth, of Reality, of God and of the unity of all being. This knowledge of God is often described in terms of love for God--the Beloved--and has inspired some of the greatest poetry of divine love in the world.

Through meditation, prayer and *zekr* (chanting the name of God), Sufis often experience the state of ecstasy, of leaving the body, of dissolving the boundaries of self. This has also been described as experiencing an altered state of consciousness or "visionary knowledge" of God, much like the mystics of Christian and Jewish tradition. Sufis speak of this state as one of "drunkenness," although of course, like all Muslims, they abstain from the use of alcohol.

To begin the study of oneself as a Sufi is to begin a journey. This inner journey must be taken under the guidance of a Sufi Master who has already completed the journey. Sufi students gather around this master, individually and as a group, for study and prayer. Most Sufis do not worship in a mosque, but gather for prayer in a home or simple prayer center called a *khanaghah.* Sufi Masters, sometimes called "Sheikhs," are prohibited from receiving any pay for their religious leadership, as Dr. Kianfar explains and demonstrates in his life.

Before a student receives "spiritual instruction from a Master, he must physically and mentally purify himself." The student must keep physically clean, correct any unpraiseworthy qualities and keep the surrounding environment clean.[6]

One of the basic principles of the teaching is discipline of the body and mind. Arriving at "a deep awareness of the Beloved and coming to understand the rule of unity requires much more than mere desire: it demands discipline and will."[7] It has been recommended by Abdullah Ansari, an ancient Sufi teacher, that a student should maintain the following: discipline of actions, of speech, of manners and of temperament.[8] The goal of discipline is balance and moderation of emotions and behavior.[9] And, of course, the discipline of steadfastness in spiritual practice is also required.

The Sufi has as the ideal leading a spiritual life devoted to God, while living a physical life within the greater society. "The treasure of Sufism . . . its principles, its teachings, poetry, music and whirling dance, its metaphors, and literature, are united and focused on the story of the limited self drawn toward the Divine."[10]

Sufism is open to those from any cultural, national, racial or religious background or faith tradition as long as they seek to know God.

WHY IS SUFISM CALLED "THE JOURNEY OF THE LOVERS"?

The Sufi journey is a path of self-transformation for those who would love to know God. On this journey students attempt to transform them-selves from their lower, physical qualities to their divine qualities. The Sufi teacher is the source of the divine energy for this transformation.

The first step on this journey is for the seeker to become aware--aware of herself and her limitations and clear in her *intention* to search for her pure inner self through meditation and prayer. The journey is a search for knowledge with a desire to know truth. In meditation students learn to concentrate their energy in their heart and find a quiet, unchanging point.

A student seeks to tame her ego and free herself from jealousy, pride, greed, hypocrisy, selfishness, arrogance and anger. She works to fill herself with praiseworthy qualities such as humility, generosity, politeness, truthfulness and contentment and to find and live from a place of balance and humility. She strives to make herself eligible to meet God. Students are instructed, "The desires of the ego extin-guish the light of love in the heart."

An essential practice of Sufism is "purification of the heart." According to an early Sufi, students are directed to "empty your heart from the attachments of the world. Whatever dwells in our heart is your beloved."[11]

As a student seeks to find and know her inner self, she embarks on a journey to enter a mystical paradise, to delight in an inner fragrance. Eventually she may enter a state known as ecstasy in which the inner self leaves the physical body and opens itself to the reality of the spirit. There she may have a personal experience of God and achieve a complete connection with the divine oneness of all existence. The goal is to lose the individual self and dissolve into unity with the wholeness of being. Through this practice, over time, a student attains a new knowledge and wisdom that is deeper than any knowledge gained in the library or the laboratory.

In the experience of unity, the heart is filled with divine love and the lover and the Beloved are one. The experience has been likened to falling in love. "There are times when the lover is so saturated by the Beloved that he forgets all else."[12] A Sufi's life is a search for the eternal essence of love in the solitude of her heart.

When a student empties herself and is filled with God, she is filled with pure love. This pure love, the love of God, is based on personal experience of God, on inner wisdom, and it is unchanging. It is not based on alternating emotions. Love that does not come from inner knowledge comes only from the wishes and desires of the ego. That love is based on emotions which are ever changing and impermanent.

Sufis are taught that:

* Love is a fire God kindles in the hearts of those who serve, and
* When you are in love with God, everyone you see is a creation of God--because there is nothing except God.

This leads to the expression of this love of God to those they meet. Sufis are traditionally known for:

* Respecting all people and all religions
* Showing hospitality to all who come to the door
* Providing service to the community by outreach to those in prison, orphans, the elderly and others in need

* Giving a percentage of their income to charity

The "Journey of the Lovers" then, is the journey of finding oneself, transforming oneself, knowing the presence of God, experiencing oneness with the Divine and being filled with divine love. The transformation has been called "the alchemy of the soul, the transmutation of base matter into pure spiritual gold."[13]

Many beautiful images have been used to describe the sacred path of Sufism.

* Sufism is the discipline of "plunging into the ebb" of a wave from Infinity and "being drawn back with it to its Eternal and Infinite Source."[14]
* Sufism leads to "the Garden of Truth, wherein alone we can realize our true identity and come to know who we are."[15]
* Sufism contains "the science and art of curing the ailments of the soul."[16]

Sufism is:

* "At the highest level a path of knowledge . . . whose highest object is the Truth."[17]

* A means for man of "integrating into his divine origin."[18]
* "Doing what is beautiful and striving after spiritual perfection."[19]

Are all Sufis the same?

There are as many Sufi orders as there are Protestant denominations, and Sufi orders differ from each other in outward form as much as Baptists do from Episcopalians. The different orders seek to experience ecstasy and unity in different ways. Some Sufi orders dance, some sing, some chant, and some are silent. The whirling dervishes are a particular order with a very special practice. What they do is called "turning" and they "turn" in divine ecstasy, filled with the love of God. They are able to perform their special practice because of their inner balance and their intense focus on the Divine. "Despite any superficial differences, the various schools of Sufism all share a common goal, to lead the practitioner to his or her actualized being."[20]

Are all Sufis Muslim?

Sufi Master Dr. Nahid Angha states, "The principles of Sufism are all based upon the rules and teachings of the Koran (Qur'an) and the instructions of the Prophet" and "all legitimate Sufi schools trace their ultimate origins back to the original group of the Prophet's spiritual disciples."[21] Sufism is wrapped within the basic message of Islam: There is nothing except the Divine.

ARE SUFIS SUNNI OR SHI'ITE (SHIA)?

Following the death of the Prophet, the division between Sunnis and Shi'ites developed regarding the succession of authority. While family members were burying the Prophet, the rest of the Muslim community gathered in Medina and selected his close follower Abu Bakr as the ruler, or caliph. This group and their followers became known as the Sunni. Some people thought the succession should be through the bloodline of the Prophet and Ali, the Prophet's son-in-law and cousin, should become the leader. These became known as the Shi'ites or Shia. Ali refused to oppose Abu Bakr and worked closely with him and the following two caliphs. In time Ali became the fourth caliph.

All Sufi orders except one believe in Ali as the one who transferred the light of the Prophet. As Seyyed Hossein Nasr says, "there are Sunnis as well as Shi'ites who are Sufis." However, he says, "these dimensions of the religion are not situated on the same level of reality." He goes on to say, "Sufism, representing the inner dimension of the religion, transcends this dichotomy."[22]

WHEN AND WHERE DID SUFISM BEGIN?

The origin of Sufism may be traced to the beginnings of Islam in the seventh century in what is now Medina, Saudi Arabia. A group of scholars gathered on the platform of the mosque of the Prophet Mohammad where he spoke, in order to discuss his teachings. They came to be called *ahle suffa* (people of the platform).[23]

These people, from many different cultures and countries, came seeking knowledge and deeper understanding. They took what they learned back to their countries, resulting in the spread of Sufism around the world. [24] Over the ages, Sufis have exerted great influence on art, poetry, music, psychology, metaphysics and theology. The most widely read poet in America today is a thirteenth century Sufi named Jelaluddin Rumi.

HOW MANY SUFIS ARE THERE IN THE WORLD? Many Sufi societies are hidden or secret, due to anti-mystical movements among some Muslims or in some countries. As one example, Turkish Sufis were suppressed by the secularist regime established there in the 1920s. Because of this, it is difficult to determine exactly how many Sufis there are. It has been estimated there are between 65 and 80 million Sufis in the world. Sufi orders are found in almost every country. Stephen Schwartz, Executive Director of the Center for Islamic Pluralism, states "I would first observe that Sufis are present, persistently, in every Muslim population."[25]

TEN IMPORTANT THINGS ABOUT SUFISM

1. It acknowledges there is one God, the source of all being, eternal and ever-lasting.
2. It acknowledges the unity of all things; all beings are part of the Divine.
3. It leads the seeker to self-understanding and encourages her to live and act from her true inner self.

4. It leads one to a deep, mystical place, outside the physical, emotional and mental realm. It is beyond words.
5. It teaches respect--for oneself, for everyone she meets, for elders, parents, and for other people's religions and spirituality.
6. It teaches gratitude and humility in recognition of the magnificence of the divine source of being.
7. It provides a place of inner balance and peace that is always accessible and shows the seeker how to get to that place.
8. It guides the student in overcoming her ego and false pride.
9. It provides guidelines for appropriate behavior and demeanor.
10. It teaches a person her essence does not die.

CHAPTER 2

What Is Islam?

❦

- *What is the most basic belief of the world's second largest religion?*
- *Do all Muslims go to Mecca on the hajj pilgrimage?*
- *How many Muslims are there in the United States?*

WHAT IS ISLAM? THE SHORT answer is that Islam is the name of a religion--the second largest religion in the world today. Islam is an Arabic word meaning "submission" or "surrender." However, Islam is actually a practice--a practice of surrendering one's whole being to the will of God. Islam requires "total surrender to the Majesty of the Absolute, before whom ultimately nothing can in fact exist. In an ordinary sense it means the surrender of ourselves to God, and in the highest sense it means the awareness of our nothingness before Him."[1] A person who practices Islam, and surrenders her will to God, is called a Muslim.

The newest of the world's major religions, Islam came into being in seventh century Arabia. It began with revelations from God received by a merchant named Mohammad who became the Prophet of Islam. The revelations became the holy book of Islam, the Qur'an. One scholar has written, "The foundation of Islam is the Koran . . . which is, for the pious Muslim, not the word of a prophet but the unadulterated word of God, which has become audible through Muhammad."[2]

The Qur'an, the sacred scripture of Islam, is "considered by all Muslims . . . as the verbatim revelation of God's word."[3] It was revealed to the Prophet Mohammed through the angel Gabriel over a period of 21 years. Numerous people memorized it and a few were appointed to write it down.

The central tenet in Islam is the belief in one God, the Absolute, the Infinite. This belief is expressed in Arabic in the testimony of all Muslims, *"La illa ha illa Allah."* This statement has been translated in several ways: There is no

God except God; there is nothing except God. The cornerstone of Islam is sincerity of faith in this "law which knows no exception."[4]

The second part of this testimony is: "*Mohammadan Rasulu 'Llah,*" which is translated as: Mohammad is His Prophet. Together these two sentences represent what is called "witnessing" or "testifying" to one's faith. It is by repeating these statements before Muslim witnesses that one becomes a Muslim. Islam is a religion of unity and witnessing, according to the teachings of Dr. Kianfar. When a student discovers her true self, she uncovers the mystery of unity, and in witnessing she becomes a messenger of God.

Dr. Kianfar says, "Islam is translated as surrender and submission to the law of God. One surrenders in order to discover the secret of unity--the unity of the whole of creation and the inner world of self. It is important to understand that the meaning of surrender or submission in Islam is not 'to obey.' . . . rather submission means to surrender your state of limitation and the illusion of separation in order to become more aware of our connection and submission to Unity."[5]

The word "Islam" is also related to the word "salaam," the Arabic word for peace, and Islam teaches peace. Muslims greet one another with the wish *Salaam aleikum* (May peace be with you).

Allah is the Arabic word for God; not the name of a different God. There is only one God, the God of Abraham, Jesus and Mohammad (peace be upon them all). Judaism, Christianity and Islam are all part of the Abrahamic tradition, all monotheistic religions, all worship the same God. Yahweh, Jehovah, Adonai, God, Allah,--all different names but the same God. All three religions honor the teachings of Abraham, Moses and David. Muslims also honor Jesus as a prophet of God.

The God mentioned "is not a being, but is a metaphor describing the entirety of existence--the Source of all Being."[6] Dr. Angha teaches that Islam brought God to the location of the human being; God is not in heaven or some-place outside the self. Muslims believe no one is separated from God; all people have a divine inner being. Dr. Angha says, "In the journey of the heart, the small identity dissolves into a greater identity, the limited self is annihilated into the greater wholeness of being."[7] Al-Moumenin Ali, the cousin and son-in-law of the Prophet, taught: "You think you are a small body, but in you is wrapped the greater world."

Social justice is a central virtue of Islam. It is impossible for a Muslim to pray to God or even think of God without awareness of this essential dimension of compassion and mercy. Allah has made clear his demand that "human beings behave to one another with justice, equity and compassion."[8]

One scholar has declared there are three levels to Islam. "On the most external level, Islam is a religion that tells people what to do and what not to do." This relates to the Islamic law. He continues, "On a deeper level, Islam is a religion that teaches people how to understand the world and themselves." This relates to faith. Finally, he says, "On the deepest level, Islam is a religion that teaches people how to transform themselves so that they may come into harmony with the ground of all being." This relates to achieving nearness to God.[9]

Today approximately 23 percent of the world's population, more than 1.6 billion people, are Muslim. Islam is the world's fastest-growing religion. According to the Pew Research Center, the largest number of Muslims lives in Indonesia, and there are Muslims in Africa, Asia, Europe, North and South America. "Five times each day . . . roughly one quarter of the earth's population prostrates itself toward Mecca."[10]

There are 7 to 8 million Muslims in the United States, and there are more Muslims in the U.S. than Episcopalians.[11] Muslims are of all races--African, Asian and Hispanic as well as Caucasian. Not all Muslim women cover their heads. It is as impossible to tell if someone is Muslim by their appearance as it is to tell if they are Methodist.

WHAT ARE THE FIVE PRINCIPLES OF ISLAM?

The five principles of Islam are the most basic beliefs and underlie the practices of the religion. They are interrelated and cannot be understood individually; they must be understood and practiced in relation to one another. "The individual accomplishes the goal of self-discovery by practicing all of the principles."[12]

ONE: THE PRINCIPLE OF UNITY

In Islam, unity means that the universe is one thing, indivisible. There is only the One; nothing but the source of all being, reality, truth, the divine essence. *La illa ha illa Allah.* (There is nothing but God.) Duality is an illusion. "Striving after the realization of that oneness . . . is the heart of Islamic life."[13]

The human being is part of the Eternal Being, and "the microcosm of the self contains within it the capacity to understand the macrocosm of Being."[14] Unity refers to "the integration of the individual soul into its center, where God resides, and then extends . . . until it encompasses the whole of creation."[15]

The Sufi student "cultivates unity in every moment" as she seeks to discover her connection to God. "Unity is the essential point of connection from the individual's heart to the eternal cosmos, God, Divine."[16] For the student, unity is the experience of being part of all creation and of all existence. It is the experience of being one with God with no separation between the creation and the creator.

Numerous scientists have documented the experience of unity in human beings. Dr. Andrew Newberg has conducted research into the neurology of consciousness and the experience of enlightenment at Thomas Jefferson University Hospital and Medical College. He concludes, "Our research shows that when people have sudden spiritual or mystical experiences, they often describe a state of consciousness where everything feels deeply interconnected." He continues, "For some, the separation between

God and one's self completely dissolves. For others, they feel a sense of absolute oneness with life, nature, or the universe."[17]

"Unity in Islam has never meant uniformity and has always embraced diversity. To understand both this unity and this diversity within unity is to grasp the way in which Islam has been able to encompass so many human collectivities, to respect God-given differences and yet create a vast civilization unified and dominated by the principle of *tawhid*, or unity."[18]

TWO: THE PRINCIPLE OF THE DIVINE MESSAGE

This principle means a human being has the potential to be in a relationship with God. When a student experiences unity, she experiences a direct connection and communication with the Divine. She is able to receive the divine message, which leads to knowledge and understanding. She understands why she is here and is able to express that understanding. She understands she is a messenger of God, and she is here to bring the message of God.

In the history of Islam there have been many prophets who have brought the divine message. "In the Islamic perspective, the oneness

of God has as its consequence not the unique-
ness of prophecy, but its multiplicity, since God
as the Infinite created a world in which there
is multiplicity. . . . The multiplicity of races,
nations and tribes necessitates the diversity of
revelations."[19]

Three: The Principle of Balance

The principle of balance is both a universal and
an individual law. On the universal level there is
balance in all creation, from the rules governing
the atom to the laws of the cosmos. Balance
in the individual is found on both the cellular
level and in the harmony among body, mind
and heart. To have unity, every element of a
person's being must be in balance in relation
to every other element. In order to experience
unity, the student must be in balance within
herself. She must find the center point that
keeps her in that perfect balance and stability.

When a person is in balance, she is in good
health and at peace. "When you reach the state
of balance, then you can experience God."[20] Pain,
illness and addictions are symptoms that appear
when the system is out of balance and unstable.
Sarah Hastings Mullin writes, "The human being

can access and experience innate divine qualities upon achieving intrapersonal balance."[21]

A seeker may find balance through:

- Silence and stillness
- Meditation
- Prayer
- Fasting
- Purification of the heart

This principle also refers to justice, which is related to balance. "The theme of justice permeates the whole of Islamic life" and the Qur'an "identifies a good society as a just one."[22] Justice is mentioned throughout the Qur'an. The Qur'an says: "God loves the just" (5:42) and "He is the best of judges." (12:80)

Four: The Principle of Guidance

Through the experience of unity, a seeker has access to guidance from within herself through her heart. The internal guide is found through the light of the spiritual teacher who can guide the student to God. When she stops looking for guidance outside herself and begins her inward journey, she may find the hidden inner wisdom that comes from God, Truth or Reality. This inner guide is the one sure and true guide and the guardian of the love of God. To find the hidden treasure, a Sufi must learn how to search within.

Dr. Kianfar instructs the student to dive into the ocean to find the pearl hidden within a hard shell under the sea. She must dive down deeply, learn how to crack open the shell, extract the pearl, and bring it up from the bottom of the sea. The teacher will teach the student how to swim, what direction to go, and how to get oxygen, so she will not get lost in the ocean. That is the point of the teacher/guide: to educate the student about her journey and lead her to find the perfect pearl within herself.

Five: The Principle of Returning to One's Origin

Scholar William Chittick describes the "return" as part of the "two journeys--from God to the world and from the world to God."[23] Another scholar, Martin Lings, says, "What is drawn back by spiritual realization towards the Source might be called the centre of consciousness. The Ocean is within as well as without; and the path of the mystics is a gradual awakening as it were 'backwards' in the direction of the root of one's being, a remembrance of the Supreme Self which infinitely transcends the human ego."[24]

For the Sufi student, the Return is accomplished by finding the light of the Divine within her heart, moving beyond time and inwardly returning to her source. In this way she reaches "the highest station of knowledge of Islam."[25]

When a Sufi has experienced unity, she finds her position and value among all of creation. She returns to her origin, to the divine oneness of all being. She is one with God. *La illa ha illa Allah.*

WHAT ARE THE FIVE PILLARS OF ISLAM?

There are five essential practices required of all Muslims, known as the Five Pillars of Islam. These practices are based on instructions received by the Prophet in the revelations from Allah that became the Holy Qur'an.

First is the profession of faith. "There is no God but Allah and Mohammad is his Prophet." This is the statement of unity, the belief in one God and the unity of all creation that is the foundation of Islam. This statement provides the follower with "discernment between the Real and unreal" in the first part, and in the second part, "the attaching of the world to God." [26]

Second is prayer. The prayer is performed five times a day. There are specific prayers for each specified time with prescribed movements of the body to accompany the words. Muslims all over the world face toward the *Kabaa* (Kabah) in Mecca while performing the prayer. The prayer may be performed alone or in a group. The intention of the prayer is to become close to God. "Pure prayer is the most intimate and most precious form of the gift of self."[27] Students are instructed that all prayer must be performed in the presence of the heart. There are additional details about the prayer in Chapter 6.

Third is giving to charity. All Muslims are required to give a portion of their wealth to charity each year. The intention of giving to charity is to serve God. Muslims share their blessings and happiness with those who are suffering from poverty, illness and misfortunes. A follower gives from a pure heart as a demonstration of faith. Islamic scholar Frithjof Schuon says, "Alms are a fasting of the soul, even as the fast proper is an almsgiving of the body."[28]

Fourth is the Hajj, the pilgrimage to Mecca. All Muslims are required to make the *Hajj* once in their lives if they are physically and financially able. The process of the *Hajj* is a means of purification. "Millions make the annual pilgrimage to Mecca during the sacred month of *Dhul-Hajja*, temporarily trading their distinctive national costumes for the anonymity of the *hajji's* white robes."[29] Pilgrims circle the *Kaaba*, the stone structure draped in a black silk cloth with gold embroidery that is the chief shrine of zIslam, as a part of the prescribed rites of the pilgrimage. "The *Kabah* (the house of God) is an established place on the earth that is the proof and symbol of the Divine. The *Kabah* was originally a place of idols but Abraham purified it and made it the house of God. A pilgrim who practices *hajj* is one who returns from the *Kabah* as a witness of the Divine."[30]

Fifth is fasting during the month of Ramadan. Ramadan is the ninth month of the Islamic lunar calendar and falls on different dates in each year of the Gregorian calendar used in the United States. It is the month in which the Prophet Mohammed first received verses of the Qur'an. The word Ramadan means "womb" in Arabic, which serves as a reminder of the cave in which the Prophet received the Holy Qur'an.

During Ramadan, followers are required to abstain from eating and drinking from sunrise to sunset unless they are ill, traveling, nursing or pregnant. The purpose of fasting is to purify the body and heart, release the follower from distractions, and help her find balance and return to her divine nature.

In the month of Ramadan, followers are urged to turn away from the world, toward the inner light of Allah. As well as fasting from food and drink, another form of fasting is to strive to prevent unknown and unwanted things from coming into a follower's hearing, sight, mind or being. During this month followers purify themselves through prayer and zekr. They are also urged to purify in the following ways:

* Clean and purify the home. Give things to charity.
* Get rid of old habits and patterns that are no longer useful. Get rid of the attraction to them. Make conscious choices about how to spend time.
* Remove the darkness from the inner system. Observe unworthy qualities and

transform them into more praiseworthy qualities. Treat others with great respect. Develop qualities of gratitude and thankfulness.

Another aspect of Ramadan is celebrating the end of the fast at sunset each day by sharing meals with family and friends. It is also a time of sharing food with others in the community, especially those in need.

EID AL-FITRA

The most important Muslim holiday is called *Eid al-Fitra* in Arabic; it is the celebration at the end of the holy month of Ramadan. Because the Islamic calendar is lunar and the Gregorian calendar is solar, Ramadan, and hence, *Eid al-Fitra,* occurs at different times of year, moving 11 days earlier each successive year on the Gregorian calendar. The celebration begins at sunset at the first sighting of the crescent moon. This is a holiday of celebration and sharing meals. Muslims traditionally wear new clothes on *Eid*, bring flowers and gifts to those they visit, and serve particular sweet dishes.

The name of the holiday, *Eid al-Fitra*, refers to the spiritual purification that Muslims strive to achieve during Ramadan: the return to the *fitra*, the original human essence created in the image of God.[31] The *fitra* is the primordial essence that existed before creation, is the origin which human beings carry within and is the source of the message of God. Dr. Kianfar teaches "the essence of the human being originates in primordial knowledge or light, and then arrives into the physical world."[32] *Fitra* is a significant concept in Islam. According to Nasr, man "is seen in Islam not as a sinful being . . . but as a being who still carries his primordial nature (*al-fitra*) within himself."[33] Dr. Kianfar also teaches that the source of the Qur'an is *fitra*.

IMPORTANT THINGS ABOUT ISLAM

1. A person who follows Islam is called a Muslim.
2. A Muslim believes that:
   - there is one God, called *Allah* in the Arabic language.
   - Mohammad is *Allah's* prophet.

3. A Muslim is someone who has surrendered her entire being to *Allah*.
4. A Muslim must practice compassion and work to create a just society.

CHAPTER 3

Who Was the Prophet Mohammad (peace be upon him)?

❦

Mohammad has been described as "one of the greatest geniuses the world has known."

❖ *Who was this orphan who was chosen to bring a new religion to the world?*

❖ *How did Mohammad receive the words of the Qur'an?*

THE PROPHET MOHAMMAD (PEACE BE upon him), is considered by Muslims to be the third and final prophet in the Abrahamic tradition, following Abraham and Jesus. (His name is sometimes spelled Muhammad.) He received the message from God that became the Holy Qur'an, went on to establish a community based on justice for all and was the founder of Islam that today is the second largest religion in the world.

Mohammad was born in Mecca, Arabia, in approximately 570 C.E. His father, Abdallah, died before he was born and his mother, Amina, died when he was only six years old leaving him an orphan. He lived with his grandfather for two years until the grandfather died, and then was raised by his uncle who was the chief of the Hashim clan.

When Mohammad was born, Arabia consisted of numerous tribes who worshiped tribal gods and idols and were in constant warfare with one another. Yet, the shrine at which all of the tribes worshiped was the *Kabaa* in Mecca. "The tribe of Quraysh, Mohammad's tribe, had been responsible for the commercial success of Mecca and they knew that a great deal of their prestige among the other Arab tribes was because they had the great privilege of guarding the huge granite shrine."[1] Belonging to the Quraysh, this ruling tribe, provided security for this young orphan.

Mohammad grew up to be known as honest and trustworthy. He became a merchant and trader and led caravans to sell goods in Syria. He was successful in business and widely respected. "The fame of Mohammad, his bravery and compassion, his honesty, perseverance and patience, and his generosity and protection of the old and oppressed, spread beyond the borders of his homeland."[2]

When Mohammad was 40, his life changed dramatically. "During the month of Ramadan in about the year 610, an Arab merchant of the city of Mecca ... had an experience that would ultimately change the history of the world."[3] Mohammad had gone to a cave on Mount Hira outside Mecca to meditate and pray. "On the seventeenth night of Ramadan when Muhammad was torn from his sleep in his mountain cave" he "felt himself overwhelmed by a devastating divine presence." The angel Gabriel commanded him to "Recite" and "he found the divinely inspired words of a new scripture pouring from his mouth. ... The holy book would be called the Qur'an."[4]

After the first revelation, the Prophet told only his wife Khadija about his terrifying experience. He went to her from the cave shaking and trembling and she held and comforted him. Ultimately, she was the first to become Muslim.

The Qur'an was revealed to Mohammad over many years. "As each new message was revealed to Muhammed . . . he recited it aloud, the Muslims learned it by heart, and those who could wrote it down."[5]

For the first three years Mohammad kept the revelations private, but he was finally encouraged to openly proclaim what he had heard and his following slowly grew. At first his followers were the poor and marginalized who responded to his teachings of respect for all. Like all prophets, he faced opposition. Many people were shocked by the suggestion of abandoning the old ways and the worship of traditional idols. He was sometimes violently attacked and many of his followers were also victimized. For two years several clans joined in a boycott against the new worshipers and refused to sell them food. Friends and relatives sent food to help them survive.

Later after the ban was lifted, political changes in Mecca made the situation even worse, and Mohammad determined he and his followers had to leave. In 622 he and a group of followers moved to the oasis of Yathrib (later known as Medina). There he established a community based on the ideals of justice and respect for all people. He was the leader of the community, its lawmaker and judge, and was widely respected for his integrity and fairness.

In Medina he built a mosque known as the Mosque of the Prophet. On the front he constructed a platform. "In fact, the first Islamic university was established on that platform, called Suffa and those who used to sit there were great, learned persons who had reached the summit of Islam, hence, they were called Ahle Suffa, the People of the Platform. The researchers connect the history of Sufism to this platform."[6]

The following years were filled with conflict, but by the time of Mohammad's death, "almost all the tribes of Arabia had joined . . . as converted Muslims." In 632 the Prophet was taken ill and died in Medina. By that time, "Single-handedly, Muhammad had brought peace to war-torn Arabia."[7]

His biographer Karen Armstrong, who is not Muslim, describes him as "one of the greatest geniuses the world has known. To create a literary masterpiece, to found a major religion and a new world power are not ordinary achievements."[8]

MOHAMMAD'S VALUES AND TEACHINGS

Mohammad lived a simple and frugal life for himself, but he was generous to his friends and benevolent to those in need.

One of the Prophet's most important teachings was the value of women. At a time of darkness and ignorance, he made women equal in everything. He told his followers the best thing one can do for God is to serve the Mother. The three most important people in his life were Amina, his mother; Khadija, his wife; and Fatimah, his daughter. He also taught if you have the resources to educate only some of your children, educate your daughters first.

The Prophet put great value on education. He proclaimed the search for knowledge was the duty of every man and woman. He was committed to social justice and compassion for all people, especially the poor, oppressed, slaves, orphans and women.

He granted religious freedom to the Jews in Medina and taught that there should be "no compulsion in religion" as stated in the Qur'an. "Muslims point out that Muhammad incorporated into his charter for Medina the principle of religious toleration. . . . They regard this document as the first charter of freedom of conscience in human history."[9]

In his last sermon he emphasized the importance of human rights and women's rights. He urged his followers to give kindness and knowledge as well as money to the needy.

This is what Gandhi said about Prophet Mohammad. "I became more than ever convinced that it was not the sword that won a place for Islam in those days in the scheme of life. It was the rigid simplicity, the utter self-effacement of the Prophet, the scrupulous regard for pledges, his intense devotion to his friends and followers, his intrepidity, his fearlessness, his absolute trust in God and in his own mission. These and not the sword carried everything before them and surmounted every obstacle." (From, *Young India*, 1924)

IMPORTANT THINGS ABOUT MOHAMMAD

1. He received the Holy Qur'an in revelations from God through the Angel Gabriel.
2. He brought the religion of Islam to the world.
3. He was a man of great personal faith and integrity.
4. He taught the honor and value of women and gave rights to women in the community he established.

CHAPTER 4

What Is the Holy Qur'an?

❧

- *What is the main subject of the Muslims' holy book?*
- *Was the Qur'an written before or after the Bible?*
- *What does the Qur'an say about women?*

Qur'an: 56:77-80 *This is indeed a Qur'an most honorable. In a Book well-guarded that none shall touch but those who are pure. A revelation from the Lord of the worlds.*

2:2 *This is the Book; in it is guidance sure, without doubt.*

12:2 *We have sent it down as an Arabic Qur'an in order that ye may learn wisdom.*

14:1 *A (Book) which We have revealed unto thee in order that thou mightest lead mankind out of the depth of darkness into light.*

THE QUR'AN, ALSO KNOWN AS the Koran, is the holy book for all Muslims. It is unique among holy books in the Abrahamic tradition (the Torah and the Bible) because it is the record of one man's spiritual experiences during his lifetime. Muslims believe the Qur'an is the culmination of the Abrahamic traditions' teachings. For Muslims the Qur'an is "not the word of a prophet but the unadulterated word of God, which has become audible through Muhammed, the pure vessel, in 'clear Arabic language.'"[1]

Mohammad first received the words from God through the Angel Gabriel while meditating in a cave outside Mecca in 610. The word "Qur'an" in Arabic means "recite" or "read." That was the first word Mohammad heard in the revelation from the angel. The words of the Qur'an were revealed to the Prophet over a period of 21 years. It was memorized by some of his companions, written down by several learned people and later compiled into a complete manuscript.

The Qur'an consists of 114 chapters called *suras* which vary in length from 3 verses to 286 verses, with a total of more than 6,000 verses. Among the chapters, "28 are revelations or specific understandings that the Prophet experienced while living in Mecca. These *suras* tend to be shorter as compared to those the Prophet experienced after his exile."[2] The chapters are arranged by divine instruction, not in chronological order, but in order of descending length. Thus, with the exception of the first chapter, the long chapters are first; the shorter chapters last.

Oral recitation of the Qur'an, as well as the five daily prayers which are taken from verses of the Qur'an, are performed in Arabic. Muslims believe the Qur'an cannot be adequately or accurately translated. Translated copies are considered interpretations or commentaries for educational purposes only. "The revelations of the Koran are presented in a style usually described as rhymed prose. The verses are not metrical, but they generally end with rhymes or similar sounds. Read aloud in Arabic, the Koran commands attention and is more powerful in spiritual impact that the mere meaning of the words can convey."[3]

It is important to realize the Qur'an cannot be understood by the literal meaning of its words and the use of the mind alone. Many of the words are metaphors or symbols that need a wise guide to interpret. Dr. Kianfar states "there is a 'veil' around the knowledge that must be lifted by mystical study."[4] Only those who have learned to understand through the heart can truly understand the message of the Qur'an, because the message exists within the individual's heart. "The meaning of the Qur'an is discovered by studying the language . . . [by the] light of the heart."[5] It is essential to have a wise teacher to direct a student in the study of the Qur'an.

The subject of the Qur'an is the human being. It is a map to help the student find herself. It is a guide to help her grow and improve, to leave behind the darkness of ignorance and the mind and find her inner light. The true meaning of the book is found within each person.

Dr. Kianfar says in *Inspirations on the Holy Qur'an*, "To study and understand the Qur'an according to the rule of Qur'an means one remains quiet, in silence, as one hears direct from God. Qur'an 7: 204: 'When the Qur'an is read, Listen to it with attention, And hold your peace that you may receive mercy.'"[6]

THE QUR'AN HONORS WOMEN
Karen Armstrong says, "The Qur'an gave women rights of inheritance and divorce centuries before

Western women were accorded such status. . . . The Qur'an makes men and women partners before God, with identical duties and responsibilities."[7] The holy book also emphasizes the importance of women and urges them to educate their daughters.

THE QUR'AN IS FILLED WITH GENTLENESS

The Qur'an in its opening lines calls God the most gracious and most merciful; likewise, the book is filled with gentleness and compassion. "The Koran, when you read it carefully, is (as) full of visions of God's wonderful gentleness toward human beings and His amazing providential care of them in every way."[8]

THE QUR'AN PROVIDES A GUIDE FOR BEHAVIOR

"For Muslims, the Quran is the source of all knowledge both outward and inward, the foundation of the Law, the final guide for ethical behavior."[9] It provides instructions for living and reveals the secret to the meaning and value of life. This is what the Qur'an says: "We have made the (Qur'an) a light wherewith We guide such of Our servants as We will; and verily Thou dost guide (men) to the Straight Way--the Way of God, to Whom belongs whatever is in the heavens and whatever is on earth." (42:52)

In describing the importance of this holy book, Karen Armstrong says, "Mohammad brought to the world a new holy book, the Qur'an, which was not only spiritually illuminating. He was also creating a new literary form and a masterpiece of Arab prose and poetry."[10]

HOW TO HANDLE THE HOLY QUR'AN

Muslims are instructed to handle the sacred book with extreme care. Followers must be physically clean and have pure intention when touching it and must treat it with deep respect. When it is closed, it must rest in a place of honor and nothing should be placed on top of it.

IMPORTANT THINGS ABOUT THE HOLY QUR'AN

1. It is the record of one man's spiritual experiences.
2. The subject is the human being.
3. It must be read by the light of the heart, not by the mind alone.

PASSAGES FROM THE HOLY QUR'AN

The reader is encouraged to read the following selected passages with an open mind and pure heart.[11]

One of the most significant passages in the Qur'an is known as the *Ayat al-Kursi*, the Verse of the Throne. This passage provides a description of God to help people understand.

2:255 *God! There is no god but He--the Living, the Self-subsisting, Eternal.*

No slumber can seize Him nor sleep. His are all things in the heavens and on earth. Who is there can intercede in His presence except as He permitteth? He knoweth what (appeareth to His creatures as) Before or After or Behind them.

Nor shall they compass aught of His knowledge except as He willeth. His Throne doth extend over the heavens and the earth, and He feeleth no fatigue in guarding and preserving them. For He is the Most High the Supreme (in glory).

The following verse is the first one received by the Prophet Mohammad from the Angel Gabriel in the cave of Hira.

96:1-5 Read! In the name of thy Lord and Cherisher, Who created--created man out of a (mere) clot of congealed blood: Proclaim! And thy Lord is Most Bountiful--He Who taught (the use of) the Pen, taught man that which he knew not.

Numerous passages emphasize knowledge, wisdom, light and wise action.

2:257 God is Protector of those who have faith: From the depths of darkness He will lead them forth into light.

2:269 He granteth wisdom to whom He pleaseth; And he to whom wisdom is granted receiveth indeed a benefit overflowing; but none will grasp the Message but men of understanding.

4:174 O mankind! Verily there hath come to you a convincing proof from your Lord: For We have sent unto you a light (that is) manifest.

6:97 It is He who maketh the stars (as beacons) for you that ye may guide yourselves, with their help, through the dark spaces of land and sea.

13:43 *Say: "Enough for a witness between me and you is God, and such as have knowledge of the Book."*

17:36 *And pursue not that of which thou hast no knowledge.*

24:35 *God is the Light of the heavens and the earth.*

24:56 *So establish regular Prayer and give regular Charity; and obey the Apostle; That ye may receive mercy.*

26:83 *O my Lord! Bestow wisdom on me, and join me with the righteous.*

31:22 *Whoever submits his whole self to God, and is a doer of good, has grasped indeed the most trustworthy hand-hold.*

55:26-27 *All that is on earth will perish: But will abide (for ever) the Face of thy Lord.*

57:3 *He is the First and the Last, The Evident and the Immanent: And He has full knowledge of all things.*

33:45-46 *O Prophet! Truly We have sent thee as a Witness, a Bearer of Glad Tidings, and a Warner,--And as one who invites to God's (Grace) by His leave, And as a Lamp spreading Light.*

Many passages offer praise and thanksgiving for the divine creation of the Earth and all that dwell on it.

2:116-117 *To Him belongs all that is in the heavens and on earth: everything renders worship to Him. To Him is due the primal origin of the heavens and the earth.*

2:164 Behold! *In the creation of the heavens and the earth; in the alternation of the Night and the Day; . . . in the rain which God sends down from the skies; . . . in the beasts of all kinds that he scatters through the earth; in the change of the winds and the clouds . . . indeed are Signs for a people that are wise.*

13:2-4 *He has subjected the sun and the moon (to his law)! Each one runs (its course) for a term appointed. He doth regulate all affairs explaining the Signs in detail that ye may believe with certainty in the meeting with your Lord. And it is He Who spread out the earth and set thereon mountains standing firm and (flowing) rivers: and fruit of every kind He made in pairs, two and two: He draweth the Night as a veil o'er the day. Behold, verily in these things are Signs for those who consider. And in the earth are tracts (Diverse though) neighboring and gardens of vines and fields sown with corn and palm trees. . . . Yet some of these we make more excellent than others to eat. Behold, verily in these things there are Signs for those who understand.*

These are some other passages important to Sufis.

2:152 *Then do ye remember Me; I will remember You.*

2:274 *Those who (in charity) spend of their goods by night and by day, in secret and in public, shall have their reward with their Lord: on them shall be no fear nor shall they grieve.*

6:79 *"For me, I have set my face, firmly and truly, towards Him Who created the heavens and the earth, and never shall I give partners to God."*

18:110 *Say: I am but a man like yourselves, (but) the inspiration has come to me, that your God is One God: whoever expects to meet his Lord, let him work righteousness, and, in the worship of his Lord, admit no one as partner.*

39:9 *Is one who worships devoutly during the hours of the night prostrating himself or standing (in adoration), who takes heed of the hereafter, and who places his hope in the Mercy of his Lord – (like one who does not)? Say: "Are those equal, those who know and those who do not know?"*

40:60 *And your Lord says: "Call on Me; I will answer your (Prayer)."*

49:13 *O mankind! We created you from a single (pair) of a male and a female, and made you into nations and tribes, that ye may know each other (not that ye may despise each other.)*

55:26-28 *All that is on earth will perish: But will abide (for ever) the Face of thy Lord, full of Majesty, Bounty and Honour. Then which of the favours of your Lord will ye deny?*

57:7 Believe in God and his Apostle, and spend (in charity) out of the (substance) whereof He has made you heirs. For, those of you who believe and spend (in charity)--for them is a great Reward.

CHAPTER 5

What Does the Qur'an Teach About Jesus?

❧

- *Is Jesus mentioned in the Qur'an?*
- *Why is there a chapter in the Qur'an named Mary?*

WHO WAS JESUS AND WHO WERE HIS FATHER AND MOTHER?[1]

THE QUR'AN WAS GIVEN TO the Prophet Mohammed as the final book in the Abrahamic tradition to describe events from the past and introduce human beings to the religion of God. However, the meaning of the Qur'an can only be obtained through the guidance of a pure teacher who knows the language of the Divine, can illuminate the true meaning and clear up any misunderstandings. Dr. Kianfar provides that guidance for students.

Muslims honor Jesus as a prophet sent by God, like many prophets before him. The Qur'an says (3:84) *We believe in God, and in what has been revealed to us and what was revealed to Abraham, Ismail, Isaac, Jacob, and the Tribes, and in (the Books) given to Moses, Jesus and the Prophets from their Lord: We make no distinction between one and another among them, and to God do we bow our will.*

The life of Jesus is presented in a very different way in the Qur'an than in the Bible. Muslims, like Christians, believe in the miracle of the divine conception of Jesus. However, the Qur'an has no discussion about the father of Jesus and states emphatically God did not beget a son.

The Qur'an says in 19:88-89, *92 They say: (God) Most Gracious has begotten a son! Indeed ye have put forth a thing most monstrous! . . . For it is not consonant with the majesty of (God) Most Gracious that He should beget a son.*

Regarding this verse of the Qur'an Dr. Kianfar states, "Because of the law of unity, God created Jesus within the principle of creation, in the same way that Adam was created." Qur'an 3:59 *The similitude of Jesus before God is as that of Adam; He created him from dust, then said to him: "Be": And he was.*

Islam is the religion of God and God cannot be divided. This unity is expressed in *La illaha illa Allah* (There is no god but God). Everything is part of this unity. Jesus was the *spirit* of God, not the *son* of God.

Islam teaches that Jesus was a human being, known in Islam as the Prophet Isa, one of many prophets sent by God. Because, as Seyyed Hossein Nasr says in a chapter titled "One God, Many Prophets," in *The Heart of Islam,* "The oneness of God is for Muslims . . . the heart of their religion."[2]

The Qur'an shows a deep respect for Mary. A chapter of the Qur'an is named after her. It is her purity that is emphasized in the Qur'an.

Dr. Kianfar says, "The discussion of 'Who was Jesus's Mother?' is far more important than the question of his father." He tells us the value of Jesus's life and teaching is based on his mother. Mary was chosen to be the mother of the Prophet Jesus because she was a pure vessel who could hold and nourish the seed of the Divine.

The Qur'an says in 3:42: *Behold! The angels said: "O Mary! God hath chosen thee, and purified thee--chosen thee above the women of all nations.*" Because of her purity, Mary's womb was chosen as the container for the spirit of God, to bring the spirit into physical form. Every person has the ability to become absolutely pure, to receive the revelation and reflect the purity of God.

In the Muslim prayer, in the posture of prostration, at one's most devout, Muslims say, in Arabic, "I praise my Lord, Thou are pure." This purity of God is only transferred to the pure. In the purest essence there is unity. The question is, how can a follower purify her heart to receive the spirit of the Divine? How can she make herself capable of becoming a worthy receiver? This is the principle for spiritual practice.

When Mary received the annunciation, she was in direct contact with God. She was not following a rabbi or any human being. She demonstrated righteous action in her total submission to the Divine.

Twentieth century Sufi Master Moulana Shah Maghsoud is quoted in Dr. Kianfar's book, *The Introduction to Religion*, "The meaning of Islam is the truthful submission of the individual to the realm of infinity."[3]

WHAT DOES THE QUR'AN TEACH ABOUT JESUS'S DEATH?

Just as the Qur'an presents different teachings about the birth of Jesus than the Bible, it presents a somewhat different account and understanding of his death. The Qur'an says in 4:157 *"They said (in boast), 'We killed Christ Jesus, The son of Mary, The Apostle of God'; But they killed him not, Nor crucified him."* Dr. Kianfar indicates that the Qur'an means that they killed only his physical body but not his soul or spirit.

Dr. Kianfar teaches that Sufis do not focus on the Christian version of the Prophet Jesus's sacrificial death with emphasis on the crucifixion. He instructs that we should concentrate instead on his life which provides the lessons for us. Jesus witnessed the truth of unity, purified himself and submitted to a loving God.

WHAT HAPPENS AFTER WE LEAVE THE PHYSICAL BODY?

The Qur'an states, *Every soul shall have a taste of death: In the end, to Us shall ye be brought back.* (29:57) According to the teachings of Dr. Kianfar, "The physical form is not capable of holding the spirit forever. The spirit passes from the physical body to another state. Just as Mary's purity allowed her to receive the command of God to bear a son, Jesus's purity allowed him to become one with divine spirit in life, so that when he left his body his soul was already in the state of pure spirit, at one with God.

"In like manner, a seeker can strive for purification in order to become eligible to receive the spirit of God, and by her submission to the will of God in her physical life, prepare herself for being united with the Divine when her spirit leaves her body.

"The quest of religion is to understand the principles that the prophets brought to us. Mary demonstrated the principles of purity and submission. Jesus also came to teach the principle of purifying the self and submitting to the will of God in order to become one with God, the Source. The emphasis of learning about Jesus should be on his admirable life rather than on his death.

"The words of the Divine are, in fact, already converted to the limitations of language. The explanations by a spiritual teacher help to release the true meaning from the limitations of common language and lead the students to clearer understanding."

IMPORTANT THINGS ABOUT JESUS IN THE QUR'AN

1. Muslims honor Jesus as a Prophet sent by God.
2. Mary was chosen to hold the seed of the Divine because of her purity.

CHAPTER 6

What Are the Basic Practices of Sufism?

❦

* *What do Sufis do besides say their prayers?*
* *Is it hard to learn to meditate?*

I. WHAT IS MEDITATION?
BACKGROUND ON SUFI MEDITATION

MEDITATION IS A MAJOR PART of the practice of Sufism. In Sufism, the true meaning of meditation is "patient concentration." Students meditate in group meetings with the Holy Masters, and it is part of their daily personal practice, performed in privacy. Practitioners sit silently, quietly and turn inward. Students are instructed to set aside a special time of day for this private practice. The Sufi Master provides each student with her own particular instructions.

WHY MEDITATE?

Put succinctly, the purpose of meditation is to experience God: a student searches to find her pure inner self, her divine center, and there to experience Unity--oneness with God. In this way, Sufi meditation is different from most other meditation practices. Dr. Angha says, "The meaning and the reason for meditation in Sufism differs greatly from attaining peaceful-ness alone."[1]

There are many reasons for meditating.

- It brings us back to ourselves, away from concerns about others, their actions, thoughts and judgments about us.
- It brings us to the present place and time, away from regrets about the past and fears for the future.
- It helps us quiet down and prepare for the divine presence.

Most people have questions about the source and meaning of life and a longing to know the truth. Meditation helps one find the answers to these questions. As a student finds her true self, as she experiences the longed-for Beloved, she discovers Reality. So, one answer to the question is that through the practice of meditation, one can find and experience the Truth, the Divine, the Source.

Also, inside every human being is a question about what will happen after the death of the body. In meditation one can find the oneness of the universe--unity with the divine source. This unity is an unchangeable state, one that does not vary or die. This part of each person existed before she came into her body, and this part will not die when she leaves her body.

WHERE AND WHEN DO SUFIS MEDITATE?

Dr. Kianfar instructs, "You need to approach this search for truth like a scientist in a laboratory--put all of your energy into it." Find a time and place when you can be quiet and alone. Turn off the computer and phone. Set aside this special time and place, and meditate at that same time and place each day or night. Many Sufis use a prayer rug for both prayer and meditation. The place must be kept scrupulously clean. This practice will take dedication and patience.

Who is there for guidance?

Dr. Angha has said, "You don't need a map to find yourself, but you do need a qualified Sufi Teacher to guide you." A student needs to search for her spiritual heart with all of her energy. "Instead of inaction, Sufi meditation consists of the essence of action."[2]

Preliminary Directions for Meditating

- Wash your hands and face and put on a clean garment you will wear exclusively for meditation and prayer.
- Sit quietly and calm your emotions.
- Quiet your mind. Stop the endless train of thoughts, going over the past, speculating, worrying and planning for the future, judging and comparing. Firmly but gently turn off your mind.
- Make yourself alone. Separate yourself from time and space. Forget everything; forget yourself, even your name. Sit still and don't move. Become empty and receptive. Have patience.
- Collect your energy from its scattered places in the outer world and bring it

back to your heart. Dr. Angha says: "concentrate all the physical, intellectual, and sensual energies in one magnetic point. In Sufism, this point is the inward heart."[3]

❀ You need to become united with yourself. That is the real meaning of meditation. Students are told, "It is YOU that you are looking for."

❀ Make yourself small--become part of the Whole, the One. Let all that is not the real you fall away. Be only light.

❀ When you find your heart, hold it through your breathing. See if you can hear your heartbeat. This will open the door of the spiritual heart. Listen to your heartbeat as a message from God. Become ready to receive the spirit. Ask God to help you.

WHAT ARE THE RESULTS OF MEDITATION?

As you continue your practice, many things will likely happen. You may find answers to your questions, guidance on what to do and how to act. You may find inspiration. You may discover an inner knowing. It can become a great help to you in your life. It may help you make peace with painful experiences, forgive, accept things as they are, life as it is. It will very likely make you stronger and healthier. It will surely help you appreciate your many blessings.

- It may calm and quiet you, lower your blood pressure, take away physical and emotional pain and help you to be more balanced and stable.
- It may lead to an experience of happiness and that can result in a higher immune function.
- It may lead to a decrease in anger and fear.
- It may cause you to experience gratitude which can lead to a transformation in your life.
- When you open your heart, you may be filled with love. You may experience love for God, for yourself and others.
- It may lead to an experience of oneness with the universe.
- Ultimately, your "heart will become capable of perceiving Divinity, hearing the divine voice and seeing the divine image."[4]

When you receive God's love, Sufis say that God, the wine bearer, pours the wine of love into the cup of your heart, and you become "the drunken one." You will hear this metaphor often in Sufi song and poetry, although, of course, Muslims abstain from wine and other alcohol.

II. WHAT IS PRAYER?

In Istanbul and Tehran and most other cities in the Middle East, the musical *azan,* the call to prayer, can be heard ringing out over the city five times a day from the mosque. Once recited by a live person chosen for this role, today loudspeakers have been installed on minarets to carry the recorded voice of the *muezzin.*

Sufis, like all Muslims, perform the prescribed prayer at specified times each day. The prayer is said in Arabic, with seven specific movements of the body to accompany the words, including bowing and prostrating with the forehead to the floor. "When carefully studying the physical movements, the body actually 'writes' 'La illa ha illa Allah' as it moves."[5]

Karen Armstrong explains, "One of the first things Muhammad asked his converts to do was to prostrate themselves in prayer several times a day. . . . The posture of their bodies was designed to teach them at a level deeper than the rational that the 'surrender' of *Islam* entailed daily transcendence of the preening, prancing ego."[6]

The prayer consists of several rounds or stanzas, and the five prayers are not all the same. The morning prayer consists of two rounds, the sunset prayer has three rounds, and noon, afternoon and evening prayers are identical and consist of four rounds each. The prayer is described in detail in *The Zekr* by Dr. Kianfar.

Dr. Mullin reports on Dr. Kianfar's teaching in *The Book of Self:* "As the practitioner prostrates in prayer, she acknowledges that everything she has she has received from God and all that she will receive will ultimately go back to God. She does not pray for any other reason than to increasingly submit to the energy of her Creator. Therefore, in Sufism, prayer is not a ritual, and it is not for God (as the Divine is self-subsisting) and it is not because one is sinful (human beings are considered innately pure in Islam), it is only for the practitioner to become increasingly aligned with her divinity."[7]

One Sufi scholar has said, "Pure prayer is the most intimate and most precious form of the gift of self."[8]

Preparation for prayer: Words from Dr. Kianfar

Make prayer your first priority. It is a great honor to sit on your praying rug and talk to the divine source. You are sitting in the presence of God when you sit on your prayer rug. You must be called by your heart not by duty. Pray from love, not asking for anything. When you pray, make a straight line from your heart to Allah.

Dr. Kianfar's instructions for performing the prayer based on his oral teachings and his book, The Zekr.

Ablution

It is required to perform ablution, or washing, to purify your physical body before prayer, as instructed in the Qur'an: "Ye who believe, when ye prepare for Prayer wash your face, and your hands to the elbows wipe your head with your hand from back to front and wash your feet to the ankle." (5:7)

Also, be sure your place for prayer is immaculately clean. You need to have both outward and inward cleanliness, so purify your mind and heart before you begin prayer. You must be in complete balance: body, mind and heart.

TIME

Prayers are said at dawn, at noon, in the afternoon, at sunset, and after twilight yet before midnight.

PLACE

Prayer must be performed in the presence of heart. Thus the inner place of prayer is the heart of the performer and the heart should remain free from hesitation and doubt. The physical place for prayer must be private and clean. It is suggested that the student perform her prayers, when possible, in the same place each time, wearing special clothing set aside for prayer.

THE DIRECTION

The performer of the prayer must face toward the *Kaaba* in Mecca. Muslims from all over the world are unified in praying toward Mecca.

CLOTHING

The clothing of the one who performs the prayer must be spotless, and she must also wear the clothing of piety, honesty, repentance and sincerity. Modesty is an important issue for Muslims, and most practicing Muslims dress with care in this regard. Some Muslim women wear head covering (*hijab*) in public although others do not. In the presence of the Holy Master, women and men cover their arms and avoid casual or sports attire. In the Uwaiysi order, Sufis wear white clothes and cover their feet with white socks for gatherings with the Holy Masters, and the women cover their heads during the actual prayer and *zekr*. The white clothing signifies that a student has been given permission to enter the Sufi order and is beginning a sacred path to come close to God. Dr. Kianfar states students are to wear the white clothing in complete honesty to show a willingness for selfless service. Students are required to perform service by teaching and demonstrating by example for those who do not understand Islam.

THE FATIHA
The *Fatiha* is the first chapter of the Qur'an, consisting of seven lines. (I:1-7) It is the beginning of the prayer each time it is performed.

Below are the Arabic words and the English translation, followed by Dr. Kianfar's explanation of their meaning.

Bes mella-he-Rahma'n-eh-Raheem
In the name of Allah, the Most Gracious and Most Merciful.

* Allah has 99 names and these are the first two mentioned in the Qur'an. (See *The Illumination of the Names* by Dr. Ali Kianfar.)
* Allah is a loving and forgiving God.
* All good things come to us through Allah's grace and mercy, not because we deserve them nor because we are worthy.
* The grace and mercy are available to us if we purify ourselves and open ourselves to receive.

Alhamdolellah-he-rabbel-a'lamin
Praise be to Allah, the Cherisher and Sustainer of the Worlds

* Allah loves all of us, his creation, and he takes care of us when we listen to him and put ourselves in a direct line to him.

A-Rahama'n-eh-Rahim
Allah is Most Gracious, Most Merciful

Maleka yo med deen
Master of the Day of Justice and Balance

- *Yo Med Deen* is the day of justice, the day of religion.
- Justice is seen as balance, so the goal is inner balance.

E ya ka naa bo dua va E ya ka nasta-ein
Thee do we worship and Thine aid we seek.

- *Dua* is our prayer, our remembrance.
- We ask God to help us always, at all times.
- We need to open ourselves to receive the light and truth from God that will guide us. We seek that light within through meditation and prayer.

Aeh denas-sera'tal mostaghim
Show us the straight way,

- The way or the path is the path of Sufism. It is the way of learning, the way of knowledge and becomes our way of living.

Seratal la zeena ana'mta alaihem, qairal magh-zoobe a'laihem va laz-zaleen

The way of those on whom Thou hast bestowed Thy Grace, those whose portion is not wrath, and who go not astray.

- We learn the way from our teachers, who have found the light and experienced Allah directly.
- It is a path of peacefulness.
- We seek Allah by making a straight line between ourselves and God.
- We seek the way that does not bring wrath from God and we seek not to have wrath within ourselves.

III. What is Zekr?

"In the remembrance of God, do hearts find satisfaction."
(Qur'an 3:28)

Zekr is the name for the repetition or chanting of certain holy names as a spiritual practice. *Zekr*, sometimes written as *zikr or dhikr*, is translated as "remembrance." Performing *zekr* often results in the experience of "ecstasy" or of leaving the body and entering an altered state of awareness.

Sufi Master Seyedeh Nahid Angha has described *zekr* in this way: "*Zekr* means remembering the Divine, as the Almighty Lord commands: 'Remember Me, so that I remember you,' or 'Ye who believe, recall God and recall Him often.' (Koran II,152; XXXIII, 41.)"[9] *Zekr* is an act of love and has been called "the prayer of the heart."[10]

Among different Sufi groups, *zekr* may refer to a variety of practices of prayer or chanting. *Zekr* may be performed individually or in a group, said aloud or silently, spoken or chanted or sung. The words are usually pronounced in Arabic and must be coordinated with the breath. However, Shah Nazar Ali Kianfar says, "The Prophet Mohammad bids that, 'It is not prayer unless it is performed at the presence of heart.'"[11] Dr. Angha elaborates, "This remembrance of God, both outwardly and inwardly, is performed in the center of the heart, and as the heart transfers its knowledge to all the body, it purifies the entire human being with its every beat."[12]

Dr. Kianfar explains that in *zekr* "the intention of the performer is to get closer to God . . . This closeness to God is achieved only when all the thoughts . . . of 'self' are eliminated."[13] In this state, the practitioner is capable of receiving the light of God. He also instructs, "To perform *zikr* properly requires perfect and pure intention and a clear focus, without distraction."[14]

Dr. Angha explains it this way: "In Sufi *zekr* (chanting) ceremonies, Sufis sit in a circle, knees side by side to the next person. The one who is the leader of the *zekr* is also sitting in that group. They all are in harmony to each other and have one common goal. The individual and the group goal is united and aimed at a harmonious understanding of the Divine . . . The *zekr* is repeated continuously and with it the group magnetic energy is connected and . . . multiplies."[15] She also describes, "When a group of people get together and form a circle of a united intention, their hearts connect and in this unified connection they begin to create an extremely powerful energy."[16]

Zekr reminds the student she is not who she thinks she is; she becomes capable of experiencing that she is one with the divine source of all being.

INSTRUCTIONS FROM DR. KIANFAR FOR SPIRITUAL PRACTICE USING THE ZEKR, LA ILLA HA ILLA ALLAH (THERE IS NOTHING BUT GOD)

Human beings have, from the beginning of time, had an inner longing--a quest to understand. But the mind has led people to look outside themselves for answers. And religions have become obsessed with this "outside" and with rituals and ceremonies.

And so people become involved with words, definitions and explanations. All that is philosophy; that is not religion. If you look inside, you will find the answers. This will tell you who you really are. You open your spirituality through practice. To practice is not to talk. Your body and your senses are just tools for your physical survival. You can transform yourself from the physical body and physical life to another realm. That is what religion is. Spiritual practice opens the door of inner knowledge and true wisdom to the human being. Amir Moumenin Ali says: "You think you are a small body, but the whole universe in wrapped within you."

How to Practice Zekr:

* Sit quietly.
* Do not move. Discipline yourself and keep your body under your control.
* Let go of the rebellion of your mind also; that is another form of discipline.
* Say out loud, but softly, **La illa ha** (There is nothing). Remove everything from yourself. Empty yourself.
* Then call on every cell in your body, from your toenails to your hair, and say, **Illa Allah** (Except God).
* Repeat the *zekr* first out loud with your tongue, then silently with your mind, and finally, use your breath to pass it into your heart.

Important Things about Sufism's Basic Practices

1. Through meditation, a seeker may experience oneness with God.
2. Prayer helps Sufi followers express their reliance on God.
3. Zekr may enable the student to have the experience of leaving her body.

CHAPTER 7

What Is a Teacher in Sufism?

❧

* *Where does one look for a Sufi teacher?*
* *Is it expensive to be a Sufi student?*

THE ONE AND ONLY TRUE teacher is Allah. A pure teacher is a representative of Allah. The teacher is a mirror who reflects the divine light and leads the student to Allah.

The important thing about a Sufi school is the presence of a wise Sufi Master whose knowledge has been passed to her or him, heart to heart, through generations of wise masters. The role of Sufi Master is passed down through initiation and appointment and is not a title that one can claim for herself or himself.

In Sufism the teacher is appointed for a student by God. Between the teacher and the student one rule always stands firm. That rule is the guidance of God governs everything, beyond any personal choice, likes or dislikes. The student meets her teacher only after she seeks and asks for a teacher. Dr. Kianfar says, "The teacher does not come and ring your door-bell." Sometimes the teacher appears when least expected and in an unexpected way. The teacher is introduced to the student through her heart by the will of God. The teacher chooses and accepts the student, not the reverse. To find one's teacher is a beautiful, deeply moving, life-changing experience for which the student feels extreme gratitude.

To be accepted as a student, an individual must be ready to accept training, discipline, guidance and instruction. According to Dr. Kianfar, as presented by Dr. Mullin, "The teacher provides instructions for the student regarding her daily physical life and later begins to focus also on the student's inner life, her meditation, her psyche, and her dream world." As the student follows instructions and stays in balance, the "spiritual energy cultivates a deep connec-tion . . . between teacher and student. Their communication begins to occur on a different plane, independent of verbalization, place or time, and often occurs when the practitio-ner is in meditation or dreaming. This dynamic becomes a relationship of love, where the practitioner recognizes a deep unity with her teacher, a friendship that is absolutely pure and genuine."[1] Ultimately the teaching is passed from the heart of the teacher to the heart of the student. The goal of the teacher is to put the student on her own path to knowledge.

A teacher never accepts pay for her or his spiritual work, nor can a student find a teacher by paying for one. Also, a student is never guided to worship a pure teacher. Neither is she guided to worship the Prophet. The student is guided to herself by the true teacher; that is the source of knowledge of the Divine. Dr. Kianfar says, "Do not go to the teacher for answers. You have the answers inside yourself. The teacher will guide you to finding your own answers." Students receive guidance through the grace of the teacher and the grace of God.

A teacher's role is to guide the student to divine knowledge. Divine knowledge is not acquired through studying, reading or memorizing, not by the use of the mind or senses but by finding the origin of divine knowledge within. Once the teacher has opened the door for the student, no one can close it.

A student begins by emptying herself completely and submitting her whole being to the teacher's guidance. She is seeking a direct, personal relationship with God. "One role of the teacher is to guide the student to purify himself to be ready to directly communicate with the Divine. The teacher acts like a mirror, allowing the student to see his impurities upon a perfect screen."[2] The student must submit her body, mind and heart to the rule of unity – there is nothing but the Divine. Under a teacher's guidance, a student begins a spiritual practice to purify her heart. It requires discipline and training that leads to her transformation. The secret of Sufism is for the student to put her head under the hands of the teacher and let her heart be free.

IMPORTANT THINGS ABOUT THE TEACHER IN SUFISM
The teacher:

* Imbues the student with inspiration
* Empowers the student to achieve things she could not achieve on her own
* Offers unconditional love, like a parent

- Provides a sanctuary for her spiritual practice
- Helps her move out of the world of change into a place of stability
- Helps her find her pure inner self
- Guides her to a place of calmness and bliss
- Becomes her companion on the spiritual journey
- Is a mirror that reflects the light of the Divine

THE TEACHER AS YOUR GUIDE

Words from Dr. Kianfar taken from
*Seasons of the Soul: The Spoken
Wisdom of Shah Nazar Seyyed
Ali Kianfar*[3]

The teacher is the companion of the practitioner from beginning to end--until you find God.

A true teacher reminds you to recognize Reality and return to yourself.

Establish the line of communication with the teacher through the heart.

The true prophet never says, "Follow me." The true prophet guides you to yourself.

Before you have a teacher, you are your own ruler. With a teacher, the king you have made of your mind is exiled and your kingdom as you know it is finished.

The teacher is a mirror without shape or form who receives the light and reflects it.

A qualified teacher is found only by a qualified student.

The teacher can show you how to develop your potential.

Who is to be our guide? The one who seeks to be our teacher, not our leader. The one who wants to liberate us, not dictate to us. The one who wants us to follow our own path.

CHAPTER 8

What Is the Purpose of Religion?

❧ *Why does a person need religion?*
❧ *Does it matter which religion a person chooses?*

Let there be no compulsion in religion: Truth stands out clear from Error: whoever rejects Evil and believes in God hath grasped the most trustworthy hand-hold that never breaks. (2:256)

THE PURPOSE OF RELIGION IS to awaken the individual to remember her divine origin. This awakening often begins with a longing or a quest to understand her place in the Universe. Not everyone experiences this; however, those who do often have a feeling there is something missing in their lives and that there is a greater unseen power they want to know. Some experience it as a desire to be close to God.

The term "religion" does not necessarily relate to "organized religion" as practiced by a specifically named group. "Religion" may be defined as an individual's search to understand herself and her connection to the Divine.

Religion is not the individual's choice; it is something inside each person, something each one is born with. Religion comes from God; it is the pure inner essence, the inner light. When a person has completely submitted to her essence, she has found her religion.

The goal of the seeker is to move into the heart and listen to the divine message with the heart. This will bring her to an understanding of her origin and her true self. This will also teach the student her value as a human being.

When the student submits to her inner wisdom, she becomes a believer. Then in every breath she is practicing Islam, submission to Allah, the One and Only. This is the purpose of religion--to move the individual out of her ego into surrender to the Divine.

The ultimate goal of the student, which many strive for but few achieve, is total annihilation of the ego and unity with the Divine, *(La illa ha illa Allah – There is nothing but God)*.

Dr. Kianfar has said that for many contemporary people, religion is like a spare tire kept in the trunk of the car, only for emergencies. Few people today are teaching about love, peace and purity--about the humanity of religion. That is what is needed in our society.

"Sheik Najmeddin Kubra, a thirteenth century Sufi, said: 'Religion is striving towards knowledge without being imprisoned by duty, obligation, and limitation.'"[1]

IMPORTANT THINGS ABOUT RELIGION

1. Religion is something inside that a person is born with.
2. Religion helps to move a person out of her ego, pride and arrogance and toward compassion and love.

CHAPTER 9

What Are Some Important Principles of Sufi Practice Taught by Dr. Angha and Dr. Kianfar?

❧

- *What does someone need to know about becoming a Sufi student?*
- *Will becoming a Sufi student require making changes?*

THERE ARE A FEW BASIC principles of Sufism requiring explanation because either the word is not familiar to English-speaking readers or the word has a different connotation or larger meaning in Sufism than in ordinary usage.

ADAB

The word *adab* is not fully translatable. It encompasses both outer and inner politeness, courtesy and respect for self and others expressed with love. It is not only how one acts but who one is inside. Adab arises from the heart and represents internal devotion. Adab includes every noble characteristic, habit, or trait that a Sufi strives for, including appropriate conduct. To have proper adab one needs humility, reverence and discipline of the ego. Adab requires respect for different cultures and religions

A student's outer actions must match her inner heart. A Sufi's behavior includes both good manners and also overcoming inferior qualities such as self-indulgence, laziness, gluttony and emotionality. She must "avoid inappropriate manners and careless qualities" and return to graciousness and an unselfish consideration of others.[1]

Adab isn't really taught or learned; it is naturally developed. Children acquire adab from their parents, students from their teachers, the young from the elders, learning from their actions. We may have much knowledge but lack adab, and we may have much adab but lack knowledge; but it is adab that holds the greater value and importance. In today's society in which parents, teachers, and elders are no longer given their correct honor, respect or rights, adab is needed.

CLEANLINESS

Before a student begins this journey, it is necessary to clean the body, mind and spirit. It begins with having a pure intention in the soul, as well as refreshing one's habits and clearing the mind of past patterns of thought. A student must, of course, practice good hygiene keeping herself physically clean at all times. She is also instructed to keep the environment clean. "The pure balance which ecology demands has been a practice ever kept sacred by the Sufis and their students."[2]

The student's mind must be free of impure thoughts, and she must carefully monitor her speech to avoid swearing or using rude or hurtful words.

Before prayer, it is required that a seeker wash hands, as well as face and feet, if possible, preparing to meet God. The area in which prayer is performed must also be kept meticulously clean.

THE HEART

Sufism teaches that the path to inner knowledge leads to the heart and away from the mind, emotions and senses. The senses assist in survival in the physical world. However, senses and emotions are ever-changing: first it's too hot, then it's too is cold. One day she is happy; the next day, sad. How can a person find stability and a reliable base under these conditions? The pleasures of the senses are also addicting, and this tends to lock a person in the body, distracted from the spirit.

The mind was designed to help with the survival of the physical body in the material world. But the mind contains information that is also ever-changing: first the mind believed the world was flat, then that it was round; first people believed that sun revolved around the earth, then the reverse. The mind holds ideas and theories, makes comparisons and is open to change as it receives new ideas. The information is often misleading. A person hears half-truths or receives information that has been manipulated by the sender. Dr. Angha says, "Information should not be mistaken for actual knowledge."[3] Often the mind grabs hold of an idea and becomes attached to it and to thoughts about it, which also distracts from the spiritual quest. The mind can play tricks and lead a person astray. The mind does not have the capacity to lead a person to stability and peace.

A Sufi student learns to access her inner wisdom from within her spiritual heart through meditation. It is through the spiritual heart that truth and reality are to be found, and they are unchanging. The heart is the source of balance and stability. It does not lie.

The spiritual heart is the center of knowledge and light. Sufis often speak of "the eye of the heart" referring to the center of one's being where the body and soul meet. The eye of the heart is the sure guide for the seeker. One Sufi scholar calls the heart "the faculty of direct spiritual . . . vision."[4] Moulana Shah Maghsoud says, "Heart is the House of God."[5] The spiritual heart is the point of connection to Allah. At this point the student can experience unity. Here she becomes the drop of water that enters the ocean of the Divine Oneness of all that is.

POTENTIAL

Each student has the potential to discover her divine nature. This is not something visible in the physical manifestation. Dr. Kianfar likens it to the potential within the seed of the apple. When looking at the seed, there is no indication it has within it the potential of becoming an apple tree.

When properly planted and nourished with soil, water and sunlight, the seed grows and develops a trunk, branches, leaves, blossoms and ultimately apples containing more seeds. Most people become so enamored with the physical appearance of the blossoms and fruit that they fail to recognize and acknowledge the energy comes from within the seed.

Just so, people become so busy with their physical life and the pleasures of the senses they ignore the immense divine power within. Individuals not only have the potential to find the divine mystery, they have the potential to become one with the power that drives the seed, the egg, and all life.

PURIFICATION

Purification is a process the student undertakes as a preparation for transforming herself into her divine nature. This concept does not involve the notion of overcoming "original sin," since Sufis believe in "original purity." However, as the pure infant comes into the physical world, she becomes mixed with people and attachments outside herself. Dr. Kianfar teaches that purification is "separating yourself from all that is not you." This process involves letting go of identification through:

* Roles based on relationships, such as wife, mother, daughter
* Roles based on career, occupation or hobby
* Cultural and familial affiliations
* Family religious traditions

A student finds her purest form through meditation and *zekr* in which she gathers all her energy and concentrates it in her heart. To achieve purification, the seeker begins by separating the physical and material aspects of herself from her spiritual essence. In order to hear the voice of the Divine, she must find her pure inner self. This has been compared to removing the diamond from the rock surrounding it. When a Sufi isolates her purest form, she experiences herself as one with the divine essence of all being. She then knows unity and is one with God. The path of purification leads the seeker to divine love and knowledge.[6]

The process of purification for students also involves:

- Examining herself honestly, admitting mistakes and making amends if appropriate
- Developing praiseworthy qualities
- Using positive energy to let go of painful memories, heal from the past and seek peacefulness
- Disciplining herself to keep boundaries and be a companion only to knowledgeable people
- Fasting during Ramadan
- Praising God through meditation, prayer and *zekr* and cultivating gratitude

According to Dr. Kianfar, "The more pure we are, the more grace and mercy we receive."

SUBMISSION

Submission is a difficult concept for many people because it suggests that one person has dominance over another. Instead in Sufism it is about surrendering the illusion of individual separation and submitting to the oneness of all existence. There is nothing but God, and no one is separated from the Whole.

Submission is the core of Islam and of Sufism. Eleventh century theologian Al-Ghazzali says, "Our free will has to be disciplined to submit to God's will."[7] As a student learns to let go of her ego and personality, she submits to her divine center. Likes and dislikes do not exist. Submission requires she become quiet and listens. When a student has the experience of unity, she is filled with divine love. When she is submitted to the Whole, she is perpetually in harmony and balance. This loving submission is the path to peace.

TRANSFORMATION

In Sufism a student seeks to transform her actions to attune to her divine nature. Transformation begins when a student is guided to see herself honestly, see her failings and work to change them. This is accomplished first through discipline of the emotions. Students are taught to avoid unworthy aspects of the ego such as anger, jealousy, pride and arrogance. Once the emotions are managed, a student can modify her behavior and act with moderation and balance, striving always to be honest, truthful, humble and modest.

Transformation is also accomplished through the practice of meditation, prayer and *zekr*. It is important to breathe in the breath of God and be filled with divine light and energy. When transformation occurs, a student lives a moral life and becomes a true human being.

SIGNIFICANT THINGS ABOUT THE IMPORTANT PRINCIPLES OF SUFISM

1. Sufism teaches that a person is born "pure" not "in sin."
2. A Sufi accesses her inner wisdom through her heart.
3. Submission to divine unity is the core of Sufism and Islam.

CHAPTER 10

What Are the Steps on a Spiritual Path?

✧

* *If a person wants to study Sufism, where does she begin?*
* *How can a seeker find inner peace?*

TO BEGIN A SPIRITUAL PATH

TO BEGIN TO WALK ON a spiritual path, or to renew the dedication to walking a spiritual path, there are certain essential steps. An individual needs to:

* Begin with a clear intention to walk a spiritual path
* Prepare to be totally honest
* Be ready to examine her life and make some changes
* Prepare to give up her attachments

- Be ready to change some of her behavior
- Create quiet, peaceful time in her daily life without distractions

FIRST STEPS ON A SPIRITUAL PATH

In order to take the first step on a spiritual path, it is essential for a student to focus on herself. Sufism teaches there is nothing but the Divine. That includes each person. Each person has a divine inner being. Each came from the divine source of all being, and to the divine source each will return. Therefore, Sufism teaches the student to look carefully at herself; honor, value and respect herself; love herself. Each person is worthy of honor.

It is important to stay grounded in the present. Dr. Kianfar tells students to stop reliving the past, feeling regrets, replaying tapes of mistake or losses or perceived slights. Similarly, stop thinking about the future with worry or projected outcomes. Stay in the "now," and take advantage of each moment of being alive.

Next a seeker must ask herself, "Am I looking for something? Is something missing in my life? Is there something I long for?" What a seeker is looking for can be found within. That is the path--the quest for inner knowledge.

This is a path one must walk alone. No one can accompany a seeker to the country of spirituality. And no carry-on baggage is permitted. In order to get there, the seeker must leave everything behind.

PRACTICES FOR SOMEONE ON A SPIRITUAL PATH
FROM DR. KIANFAR
Examine your present life:

* Do you have peace and tranquility in your life? If not, what disturbs your balance and peacefulness?
* Are you often annoyed and irritated? Do you feel pressure and stress? Are your emotions out of control?
* Do you worry about what other people think of you? Do you often compare yourself to others?

Strive to achieve inner peace. The following steps will help you on the road to creating inner peace:

- Make yourself your top priority. Put yourself first.
- Set a quiet time for yourself each day. This time should be without media, without other people, in a place where you can be absolutely alone.
- Start with 15 minutes each day of meditation. Turn off your mind and open your heart. Make space for God, and ask God for help.
- Follow good health practices by eating a balanced diet of pure food, getting enough sleep on a regular schedule, and including exercise in your schedule.
- Find activities that help you maintain inner balance and stability.
- Appreciate the gift of your life and your many blessings. Express gratitude for food, clothes, shelter; for health, for friends and family; for friendship and love, for the beautiful Earth.

Eliminate harmful thinking and practices:

- Re-organize your calendar to make more time for yourself. Eliminate some activities and obligations. Change some of your identifications.

- Stop keeping busy with other people, their lives, and their problems.
- Stop worrying about what other people think of you, your actions, your decisions, and your life.
- Control your emotions with breathing practices, meditation and physical exercise.
- Stop judging yourself and others. Substitute compassion and acceptance for judgment.
- Tame your ego: Avoid thinking of yourself as superior, entitled, right.

Remember this saying: You can be right or you can be at peace.

- Avoid envy, pride, jealousy, anger, vanity, arrogance, dishonesty, gossip, resentment, greed, blame, criticism, prejudice, argument.

Cultivate praiseworthy qualities:

- Humility, politeness, piety, honesty, loyalty, reverence, patience, tolerance, gratitude
- Respect for yourself
- Respect for others, their beliefs and their religion

* Compassion for yourself and others
* Acceptance of life as it is and others as they are

The spiritual path requires discipline and constancy. This is not something to which you can drop in and drop out. This path is the Sufi's connection with the Divine. Sufi Master Moulana Shah Maghsoud says, "The only thing I know is that a person who is not busy with others is one who recognizes the truth of existence."[1]

IMPORTANT THINGS ABOUT A SPIRITUAL PATH

1. A person must walk the spiritual path alone.
2. On the spiritual path, a student must focus on herself, not on others
3. A spiritual path requires discipline and constancy.

CHAPTER 11

What Are the Physical Culture and the Divine Culture?

❧

* *Does God cause suffering?*
* *Should we always put others first?*

DR. ANGHA AND DR. KIANFAR teach that the condition of the human being is that she struggles between two cultures: the physical culture and the divine culture. The physical culture is limited to the body and is easily seen, while the divine culture is hidden within and a person must seek to find it.

GOOD AND EVIL

If, at the core, the human being is one with the Divine, she must be, at the core, in her origin, good and pure. But the human being also has the ability to ignore her divine nature and live only on the physical plane. She has the ability to commit wrong actions. It is up to each person whether or not she searches for her divine nature.

Evil and suffering in the world are not the fault of God, nor caused by God, nor willed by God. Evil is the fault of human beings living only in the physical culture. It is the actions of people that cause suffering. Viktor Frankl says of his experience in the German concentration camps, a person always has the choice of how to act and how to react to any situation.[1]

In Sufism, our goal is to transform our actions to attune to our divine nature. This is done through:

- the disciplines of truthfulness, humility, moderation and balance.
- the practices of meditation, prayer and *zekr*

OBSTACLES TO LIVING IN THE DIVINE CULTURE
What most children in our culture are taught by parents, teachers, in Christian Sunday School, Girl Scouts and others is: ***put others first***. This may be the primary obstacle to finding one's own

true self and living in the divine culture. In fact, an individual needs to make herself her number one priority. As Dr. Angha relates, it is like being on an airplane with a child when the pilot instructs the adult to put on the oxygen mask first and then help the child. Dr. Angha is not suggesting we escape into ego, rudeness, vanity and greed. Rather, the student is to use discipline and spiritual practice to find her divine self and then be able to serve others with an honest, open heart.

Our society puts so much emphasis on satisfying the senses in the moment: eat, drink and be merry. **Putting the senses first** is another obstacle to face. The body is a tool, designed by God, necessary for our physical survival. It may be used to meet the needs of our physical life, or it may be used for the divine purpose of achieving knowledge and wisdom.

When a person approaches another with expectations, she is so often disappointed and falls into negative emotions. **Expectations of others** are products of the mind; they do not come from the heart. They are illusions. Instead, a student is guided to:

* stay in the present moment
* accept what is

- accept people for who they are
- meet and see each person with love

One of the major challenges to living a spiritual life is taming the ego. In a competitive culture, the individual is constantly encouraged to be first, to be best, to win, to be famous, and to be popular. A person is lured into **serving her own ego** by taking pride in temporary, physical achievements such as in sports or attributes such as in beauty. Instead the teachers guide students to have humility before the source of all being and to become a servant of God.

The mind poses a great obstacle for the spiritual seeker with its habit of judging. The student is constantly **judging herself and judging others**, making comparisons rather than having compassion. Relevant questions to ask oneself are:

- Who am I to judge?
- Who would I appoint to judge me?

What is needed is love and humility. Leave the mind behind. Sufism teaches the seeker to see the Divine in oneself and see the face of God in everyone she meets.

HUMILITY AND SUBMISSION TO THE DIVINE AS A PATH TO KNOWLEDGE

The beginning of submission is humility, and the beginning of humility is to admit, "I know nothing" before the source of all being. This "I" is the "I" of the ego and the mind. The universe is vaster and more complex than anyone can comprehend or explain. The Creator who designed it and keeps billions of galaxies in order is beyond our understanding. How can a person be anything but humble?

Much of what happens in life is beyond the control of the individual: personal health, one's children's health, the health and well-being of family and loved ones. Only the very young think they are invincible and will be happy and healthy forever.

What, then, is the path to submission?

* Stay in the present.
* Do not relive the past and wallow in guilt for what has been done. It is necessary to begin to transform one's life.
* Do not become addicted to going over and over painful images and memories from the past
* Do not imagine the future and live in fear.

* Accept what is--what is the choice? The only choice is in one's attitude. As Frankl says, the choice is in how we act and react.
* The heart is the place where the student finds her pure self.
* When she submits to her pure self, she submits to God because *La illa ha illa Allah* (There is nothing but the divine source).

IMPORTANT THINGS ABOUT THE DIVINE CULTURE

1. The human being is good at her inner core.
2. The human being must search to find her divine nature.
3. Humility is the beginning of submission to one's divine nature.

CHAPTER 12

What Guidance Have Dr. Angha and Dr. Kianfar Provided for Students?

❧

- *Are there tips for getting started?*
- *Is it necessary to make new friends?*

Stop being busy.

Make yourself empty to receive the light.

Keep tranquility and peace in your life. Turn away from what is disturbing.

Accept all of life as it comes from God. See whatever is happening through the eyes of love. Do not judge.

Do not give so much of yourself away.

Every thought, word and action can be a *zekr*, a remembrance.

Ask God for guidance.

Be quiet and listen.

Find the divine melody in yourself.

Hear only what is inside; see only what is inside.

Separate yourself from society.

Your goal is to be close to the Divine.

Choose your companions carefully. Your friends represent your beliefs. You may need to make new friends.

When you are in the center of a storm, hang on to something strong and be patient. The storm will pass.

Do what gives you inner balance and stability.

Stop being concerned with other people's lives.

Express gratitude daily.

Stay in the present. Stop thinking about the past and worrying about the future.

Control your emotions.

Stop judgment of yourself and of others.

Make peace with yourself.

Stop worrying about what other people think.

Respect others--all people, their beliefs and their religion.

Practice compassion.

Give up unpraiseworthy actions and practices.

Become quiet to hear the voice of the Divine.

You will find the Divine within yourself.

Treat everyone with kindness and respect.

Don't correct others; correct yourself.

Release yourself from any situation that is not pulling you to health, peace and love.

IMPORTANT GUIDANCE FOR STUDENTS

1. Treat everyone with kindness and respect
2. Practice compassion

CHAPTER 13

Are There Other Questions To Be Answered?

❧

- *Why are we here?*
- *Is death a gateway to something else?*

THOSE INTERESTED IN SUFISM FREQUENTLY ask some of the following questions.

WHY DID GOD CREATE THE WORLD AND HUMANKIND?

Dr. Kianfar points to the saying of the Prophet, "I was a hidden treasure, and I desired to be known," which teaches that God created man out of love.

Twelfth-century Islamic scholar Ibn Al 'Arabi answers this question by quoting the Qur'an: "I did not create jinn and men except to serve me." (51:56) He says, "Here by *jinn* is meant everything hidden."[1] He also says, "God created the creatures to worship Him."[2]

WHAT ARE SIN AND HELL?

In Islam, sin is whatever prevents a person from seeing the light of God. Sin is being out of balance and clouded by ignorance. Sin is believing it is possible to be separated from God. Sin is forgetting that at her inner being, a person is one with God, the source of all being; she came from God and to God she will return.

Hell is being cut off from God. It is a state of being trapped in the physical life, filled with uncertainty. Hell is change, lack of constancy.

WHAT IS JIHAD?

This term has been much misunderstood and misrepresented by the media in recent times. The Arabic word *jihad* may be translated as exerting effort; striving or struggle. It is not a call for war. The Qur'an forbids killing the elderly and children under any circumstances; killing anyone is permitted only to defend oneself and only when clearly attacked. Sufism is concerned with the "inner *Jihad*"--the student's inward striving to transform herself into a better person. It refers to the effort one asserts to serve God.

Dr. Amineh Pryor says in *Sufi Grace,* "This effort and striving is an integral aspect of the practice and psychology of Sufism."[3] She goes on to say, "The striving or exertion within is to overcome any instability, shadow, or clouded intention and to work continually to realize the Divine within and to understand, through experience, the unity of existence."[4]

Each student is called to her own inner *jihad,* striving to:

*   Overcome her ego
*   Purify herself from all except her true self
*   Transform her undesirable qualities into good qualities
*   Cultivate outward and inward peace.

"Within Sufism," Dr. Pryor continues, "it is understood that this effort toward awareness and betterment is a lifelong commitment because of its enormity. Essentially, we are striving through this psychological effort to overcome the weakness of our egos and to transform or even to transcend our personalities."[5]

IS THERE LIFE AFTER DEATH?

In his introduction to *Inspirations on the Holy Qur'an,* Dr. Kianfar states, "Life is one continuum, no beginning or ending, no past or future, only different stages and states of being. Even death, that major event in the life of human beings that everyone, without exception, experiences, is not a sudden finality but is, in fact, a gate through which we pass from one level to another. Our physical life is but a part of this continuum that extends far beyond the borders of our individual life span."[6]

Dr. Kianfar teaches that all shapes, forms, colors and energies in the universe are based on one thing, one essence. We call this essence God. The essence is the first and last, beginning and end. That is why we do not die, because we are one with this essence.

Sufis use the phrase, "die before we die." This refers to the attempt to overcome the ego and submit completely to the Divine, to leave behind the small self and move into unity with all of existence. Al Moumenin Ali said, "You think you are a small body, but in you is wrapped the greater world."

Important things about these questions

1. Sin is forgetting that a person cannot be separate from God.
2. In Sufism, *jihad* refers to a student's attempt to transform herself.
3. Life does not necessarily end with the death of the physical body

CHAPTER 14

What Is the Uwaiysi tariqat and Who Was Uwaiys al Qaran?

❧

*   *Where did the Uwaiysi order begin?*
*   *What makes this order unique?*

AS EXPLAINED PREVIOUSLY, THERE ARE many different Sufi schools or orders, and though some of their practices differ, they are all based on the inner teachings of the Qur'an and share the same basic goal of guiding the practitioner to experience her inner self in unity with the Divine.

The origin of Sufi orders begins, of course, with the Prophet. "Every Sufi order goes back to the Prophet and through him and the archangel Gabriel to God."[1] However, a Sufi order or school (*tariqat*) is usually identified by the name of the Sufi Master who founded it. Uwaiys al Qaran lived at the time of the Prophet but never met him. "Uwaiys was a direct follower of the Prophet who received, by his heart, the meaning and essence of the Prophet's message."[2] The Prophet recognized that Uwaiys had received his knowledge, and when Mohammad was dying, he ordered that his robe be sent to Uwaiys. This began the order of the unseen teacher who communicates with followers heart to heart. There have been many Uwaiysi schools in the intervening years.

Moulana Shah Maghsoud, 20th century Persian Sufi Master of the Uwaiysi tariqat established his *khanaghah* in Tehran and then in Sufi Abad. His school has followed the way of Uwaiys, with knowledge of the Divine received through the inner teacher present in the heart. His teachings are based upon the unification of spirituality and science, using scientific analysis and principles to establish a truthful understanding of religion--a true understanding of Islam, the foundation of Sufism."[3]

Moulana Shah Maghsoud Angha, born in 1916, was educated in law at the University of Tehran and studied spirituality under his father, the noted Sufi, Hazrat Mir Ghotbeddin Mohammad Angha. Moulana Shah Maghsoud wrote many books on spirituality, science and philosophy, as well as poetry, most of which have been translated into English by his daughter, Seyedeh Nahid Angha. In addition to being a well-known and respected Sufi Master in Iran, he traveled widely, giving lectures in numerous other countries.

In the 1970's, Moulana Shah Maghsoud brought his teachings and his family, including his daughter and her husband, Pir Maghsoud's long-time student, Shah Nazar Seyed Ali Kianfar, to the United States. After his death in 1980, his teachings have been continued by many of his students including his daughter Dr. Angha and her husband Dr. Kianfar, both of whom he appointed to teach. They now have numerous students in many parts of the world.

IMPORTANT PRINCIPLES IN THE TEACHINGS OF MOULANA SHAH MAGHSOUD

1. The teachings are based on the unification of science and spirituality.
2. His teachings have been made available to students in this order around the globe.

CHAPTER 15

What is the International Association of Sufism?

❧

* *Where is this organization based?*
* *Who are its leaders?*

THE INTERNATIONAL ASSOCIATION OF SUFISM (IAS) was founded in 1983 by Sufi Masters Seyedeh Nahid Angha, Ph.D. and Shah Nazar Seyed Ali Kianfar, Ph.D. The headquarters of the organization are in Marin County, California. IAS is a non-profit, humanitarian organization and a non-governmental organization (NGO) of the United Nations' Department of Public Information. It was formed to:

* introduce Sufism to the public
* create and provide a global forum for a continuing dialogue among Sufis, scholars,

      interfaith leaders, poets and artists from diverse cultures, nations and schools

* bring together Sufi principles and scientific understanding
* promote equality and human rights

IAS has played a significant role in promoting interfaith dialogue and understanding in California and internationally. IAS has been an important part of interfaith activities in Marin County and at the Interfaith Center at the Presidio in San Francisco. Dr. Angha has had a leadership role with United Religions Initiative, the Parliament of the World's Religions and the Institute of the World's Religions. She participated in the National Interreligious Leadership Delegation and the United Nations Millennium World Peace Summit of Religious and Spiritual Leaders. IAS was given the Messenger of Peace award from UNESCO in 2000.

The IAS consists of the international organization as well as a school of students from throughout Northern California who meet regularly with the Sufi Masters in gatherings at the Sufi Center in Novato. In addition, with modern technology, followers from around the country and the world join the gatherings via Skype.

IAS DEPARTMENTS

The IAS has numerous departments, including the following:

- **The Sufi Women's Organization** is an international humanitarian organization founded by Dr. Angha. It brings together Sufi women from across the world through online publications and dialogues, conferences, retreats and regular meetings in Marin County to address human rights and women's rights issues. SWO also promotes women's artistic endeavors, provides education and participates in social service projects.

- **Taneen Sufi Music Ensemble** consists of musicians who blend Western and Middle Eastern instruments with authentic translations of Sufi poetry and chants to create a unique sound. They perform regularly in California, across the United States and throughout the world. They have released several CDs.

- **Avay-i-Janaan: Echoes of the Unseen,** a poetry slam collective, synchronizes rhythm and movement with words and music. They lead the listener on a path to inner peace.

- **Voices for Justice** is a group of youth and young adults who advocate for the rights of children to fulfill their highest potential. They provide education, advocacy, community service, and support for UNICEF.
- **Community Healing Centers** in Marin County and San Francisco offer counseling and psychotherapy provided by licensed therapists, as well as workshops and public programs. They blend Sufi healing practices with Western psychotherapy.
- **The Prison Project** provides correspondence, books and journals to inmates in jails and prisons throughout the US, promoting individual responsibility and increased self-understanding. Over the past 20 years, IAS leaders have offered meditation and other workshops for inmates in several jails and in San Quentin prison in the San Francisco Bay Area.
- **The Institute of Sufi Studies** offers a variety of classes, meditation groups and retreats for people of all ages at its Novato center.

IAS PROGRAMS

- **The International Sufism Symposia,** for the past twenty years, has brought together Sufi and interfaith scholars and leaders from around the world with artists and musicians to share wisdom and celebrate together.

- **The Forty Days: Alchemy of Tranquility program** offers day-long and weekend retreats led by Dr. Kianfar, assisted by psychotherapists and educators. The programs help students deepen self-understanding and engage in spiritual development. These retreats are followed by sessions designed to assist students in developing their personal practice over a 40-day period.

- **Building Bridges of Understanding** is an educational program provided in cooperation with the Humanities Department of Dominican University of California, located in San Rafael. For more than 15 years, scholars, religious and community leaders have given lectures and presentations in day-long workshops open to the university and the community.

The programs have provided education about the major religions of the world, as well as contemporary issues.

IAS PUBLICATIONS
IAS has published the journal, *Sufism: An Inquiry* for more than 20 years, formerly in print, now online at www.sufismjournal.org.

The IAS also publishes numerous books and produces video and audio CDs.

IMPORTANT THINGS ABOUT THE INTERNATIONAL ASSOCIATION OF SUFISM (IAS)

1. IAS promotes interfaith dialogue and understanding.
2. IAS is a non-governmental organization (NGO) of the United Nations' Department of Public Information.

CHAPTER 16

Who are Seyedeh Nahid Angha and Shah Nazar Seyed Ali Kianfar?

❦

- *Is a Muslim woman really in a leadership role?*
- *Where are these wise, world-renowned leaders to be found?*

SEYEDEH NAHID ANGHA

SEYEDEH NAHID ANGHA, PH.D., IS co-founder and co-director of the International Association of Sufism (IAS), founder of the Sufi Women Organization and the executive editor of the journal *Sufism: An Inquiry.* An internationally published scholar, she has lectured at the United Nations, the Smithsonian Institution, the Parliament of the World's Religions, UNESCO and many other organizations. She was among the distinguished Muslim leaders and scholars invited to the first Shakir World Encounters in Marrakech, Morocco, and she is the first Muslim woman inducted to the Marin Women's Hall of Fame. Huffington Post named her one of the 50 Powerful Women Religious Leaders to Celebrate on International Women's Day, 2014.

She is recognized world-wide for her leadership as a Sufi teacher, scholar, and advocate for human rights and the rights of Muslim women. She is the author of 15 books and many articles, and is one of the subjects of the books, *Women of Sufism* and *Hope and Healing in a Troubled World.* Under her direction, IAS became a non-governmental organization of the United Nations' Department of Public Information, and she is the main representative of the IAS to the United Nations.

Dr. Angha is notable for having established the Sufi Women's Organization, a forum for Sufi women from all Sufi orders, which is dedicated to humanitarian work worldwide. She has been instrumental establishing the many departments of IAS and developing a partnership with Dominican University of California to produce the Building Bridges of Understanding 15-year educational conference series.

Dr. Angha was appointed by her father, Sufi Master Moulana Shah Maghsoud Angha, to lead Sufi spiritual gatherings in the late 1960ties in Iran and since 1985 has been leading gatherings in the US. She is the mother of two daughters and has one grandson.

Shah Nazar Seyed Ali Kianfar

Sufi Master Shah Nazar Seyed Ali Kianfar, Ph.D. is beloved by his many devoted students in Northern California, across the U.S. and throughout the world, and respected and honored internationally for his knowledge and wisdom. He was appointed to teach in the Uwaiysi tariqat by Sufi Master Moulana Shah Maghsoud Angha in Iran. After coming to the US in 1983, he and his wife co-founded the International Association of Sufism and continue to serve as co-directors. Together they developed, and for the past twenty years have led, the International Sufism Symposia.

An internationally published author, Dr. Kianfar has also been the editor-in-chief of the journal *Sufism: An Inquiry* for more than 20 years. He has taught and lectured on Sufism, Islamic philosophy and the Qur'an around the world at colleges and universities, at the United Nations and on public stages with other spiritual leaders including the Dalai Lama. He was the keynote speaker at a UNESCO conference on

Interreligious Dialogue and Peace in Tashkent, Uzbekistan.

Dr. Kianfar has held traditional Sufi gatherings throughout the United States, in Europe and the Middle East and together with Dr. Angha leads regular spiritual gatherings with students at the Novato Sufi center. His students from throughout the United States and in other countries attend these gatherings through electronic media. He also developed and leads the 40 Days: Alchemy of Tranquility program, a Sufi-psychology curriculum integrating Western psychology with Sufi mysticism.

Dr. Kianfar is renowned for his honorable life, adherence to the principles of Sufism, his knowledge, wisdom and kindness.

IMPORTANT THINGS ABOUT DR. ANGHA AND DR. KIANFAR

1. Dr. Angha is the first Muslim woman inducted to the Marin Women's Hall of Fame.
2. Dr. Kianfar developed and leads the 40 Days: Alchemy of Tranquility program integrating Western psychology with Sufi mysticism.

CHAPTER 17

Who Are Some Other Significant Muslim and Sufi Women?

⟳

* *Who is the most famous female Sufi saint?*
* *Who is the first Muslim woman to win the Nobel Peace Prize?*

THE WIFE OF THE PROPHET
KHADIJA BINT KHUWAYLID, 6TH CENTURY

Khadija was the first wife of the Prophet, his only wife for 25 years until her death, and the only one to bear his children. "Before marrying Muhammad, she had been widowed, and had developed and been conducting her own business in caravan trade. She was forty years old, when, being aware of Muhammad's sincere trustworthiness and skillfulness, she hired him to oversee one of her caravans."[1] After his success in his work for her, she proposed marriage to him and he accepted. They had a happy and loving marriage. It was she who comforted him when he came to her trembling after receiving the first revelation. She was the first to have faith in his prophecy and embrace Islam.

THE DAUGHTER OF THE PROPHET
FATIMA AL-ZAHRA, 7TH CENTURY

Hazrat Fatima was the daughter of the Prophet and Khadija. Dr. Pryor says, she is "held in reverence and respect as a strong, well-educated woman who stood for her rights and the rights of others."[2] She married the cousin of the Prophet, Al Moumenin Ali, and they had four children. Her two sons became the first two Imams of the Shi'ite sect. She died in her twenties after the death of her father. Following his death, all belongings given to her by her father were taken away by the Caliph Abu Baker. Yet, she bravely stood up for her rights. "It was during this brief time at the end of her life that she made one of her most moving speeches to the Caliph and the people."[3]

AN EARLY SUFI SAINT
RABI'AH AL-ADAWIYYAH, 8TH CENTURY

"Rabia of Basra is without a doubt the most popular and influential of female Islamic saints and a central figure in Sufi tradition." She was known for her intense devotion to God. Despite many trials in her life, she wrote "whatever happens is bringing us closer to God."[4] Many miracles are attributed to her, and her sensual poetry continues to be widely read today.

A 21ST CENTURY NOBEL PRIZE LAUREATE
SHIRIN EBADI

Shirin Ebadi, an Iranian lawyer, writer, activist and dissident, became the first woman to win the Nobel Peace Prize. As one of the world's leading human rights activists, she received the award in 2003 for her extensive efforts to promote human rights and the rights of women, children and political prisoners in Iran. She was the first woman judge in Iran and was removed at the time of the Revolution. However, she continued her career as an attorney, professor and scholar and became known for defending the disenfranchised. She has been harassed and humiliated, persecuted, imprisoned in solitary confinement and survived assassination attempts in response to her brave advocacy. Today she lives in exile. She is the author of several books and lectures widely in the West.

IMPORTANT THINGS ABOUT THESE MUSLIM AND SUFI WOMEN

1. Khadija, the first wife of the Prophet, was the first person to embrace Islam.
2. Nobel laureate Shirin Ebadi was held in solitary confinement for her human rights advocacy in Iran.

CHAPTER 18

What is Sufi Poetry?

❧❧❧

❧ *Why are Sufis famous for poetry?*
❧ *Was Rumi a Sufi?*

ONE PRACTICE THAT HAS BEEN central to Sufism for 1400 years is Sufi poetry. This remarkable poetry attempts to convey the ecstatic love of God. As Sufis seek their hidden inner essence, so their poetry relies on often allusive symbolism. First of all, the seeker is the lover and the God is the beloved. As Sufis believe that when they are filled with divine love they are purified, so in Sufi poetry the fire of divine love burns the lover and purifies her. The Sufi poets also describe the experience of ecstasy, being filled with divine love and leaving the physical body behind, through imagery. The seeker comes with an empty cup, her heart, and waits for the wine bearer, the Divine, to fill her cup with the wine of love. Then she becomes "the drunken one." This imagery has led to many misunderstandings because Muslims do not use alcohol.

In her book *Ecstasy: The World of Sufi Poetry and Prayer*, Dr. Angha says, "Sufi poets bring an extraordinary contribution to both the world of religion and the world of literature. To many, these worlds may seem very different--the one, universal, the other, highly personal. Yet in their love poems for Allah these two worlds come together in the unity of divine love. "[1]

Dr. Angha continues, "The portrait of the Sufi's Beloved is so magnificent that one falls in love with the beauty of the Beloved, a Beloved hidden within and behind the world of nature. Sufi poets constantly create magnificent works of ecstasy in their glorification of the divine message. Their poetry becomes a manifestation of the Beloved, Allah."[2]

SOME BEAUTIFUL SUFI POETRY
From **Moulana Shah Maghsoud**, 20th century Sufi (see Chapter 14)

"Pure springs rise out of the heart of the earth; they flow even through the barrens of harsh rocks, and their courses are not obstructed by mud . . . The shadow of gods is cast, like a cloud, over the earth, and its rains pour upon the soil. It increases the fertility of land that is ripe. The highlands shed water from their soil, but the valleys and ponds are filled with it, they grow trees bearing fruits and foster fish. Yet the rebels do not learn from those humble ones." [3]

From **Rabia**, 8th century Sufi, (See Chapter 17)

"The sky gave me its heart because it knew mine was not large enough to care for the earth the way it did. Why is it we think of God so much? Why is there so much talk about love? When an animal is wounded no one has to tell it, 'You need to heal'; so naturally it will nurse itself the best it can. My eye kept telling me, 'something is missing from all I see.' So it went in search of the cure. The cure for me was His beauty, the remedy--for me was to love." [4]

From **Ezzeddin Nasafi**, 13th century Sufi

"Ezzeddin Nasafi was one of the Sufi scholars of thirteenth century Persia whose book, *Insan-e-Kamel,* has been considered one of the major texts for Sufi studies."[5]

> *"Oh, my friend: Love makes the world of creation a possibility and the ecstasy of ascension a will. Look around yourself and see a universe saturated by the fragrance of love. . . . If you are a person of the inner path, then you are a person of peace, so make peace with yourself and your surroundings. "*[6]

From **Jelaluddin Rumi**, 13th century Sufi

Jelaluddin Rumi was born in Eastern Persia (now Afghanistan) and raised in Konya, Turkey. He was a "fairly normal" Sufi Sheikh, teacher and scholar until making an ecstatic connection with Shams of Tabriz. His poetry reflects his love for and divine union with Shams. One of the great Sufi mystical poets, today Rumi is the most widely read poet in the English language.[7]

"All religions, all this singing, Is one song. The differences are just illusion and vanity. The sun's light looks a little different on this wall than that wall, and a lot different on this other one, but it's still one light. We have borrowed these clothes, these time and place personalities, from a light, and when we praise, we're pouring them back in." [8]

"All day I think about it, then at night I say it. Where did I come from, and what am I supposed to be doing? I have no idea. My soul is from elsewhere, I'm sure of that, and I intend to end up there. . . . I didn't come here of my own accord, and I can't leave that way. Whoever brought me here will have to take me home." [9]

"Essence is emptiness, everything else, accidental. Emptiness brings peace to loving. Everything else, disease. In this world of trickery emptiness is what your soul wants."[10]

"If God said, 'Rumi, pay homage to everything that has helped you enter my arms,' there would not be one experience of my life, not one thought, not one feeling, not any act, I would not bow to."[11]

"The light of God is an ornament of wisdom. That is the meaning of 'light upon light.' The light of reason draws toward the earth. The light of God carries you aloft. Things of reason are of the lower world. The light of God is an ocean, reason merely a dewdrop."[12]

"Oh, lovers: let deception depart, Come and join the drunkard. Rise from the heart of fire to become a butterfly, one foot upon your ego, the other on the world. Then and only then may you seek refuge in the house of the drunkard. Purify your heart, cleanse your soul, leave your jealousy, ill will and all: Then and only then become a Cup for the Wine of Love. Turn into life deserving of the Beloved if you would journey towards the house of the Wine Bearer: Come Drunkard."[13]

From **Hafiz,** a 14th century Sufi

"Shams-udo-din Muhammad Hafiz (c. 1320-1389) is the most beloved poet of Persians and is considered to be one of history's greatest lyrical geniuses."[14] He wrote mostly short poems expressing feelings for his Beloved. He often sang them and many still sing them today.

"Do you know how beautiful you are? I think not, my dear. . . . Speak to me of your mother, your cousins and your friends. Tell me of squirrels and birds you know. Awaken your legion of nightingales--Let them soar wild and free in the sky, And begin to sing to God. Let's all begin to sing to God! Do you know how beautiful you are? I think not, my dear." [15]

"A field of flowers, a Cup of Wine, and the Beloved by my side, with such wealth, the king is my servant tonight."[16]

"Oh morning breeze tell me, Where is the Beloved resting? Where is her dwelling, she who melted all so many hearts? . . . I long for You. Every bit of

my being longs for You. I am here, anni-hilated in You."[17]

From **Moulana Shah Maghsoud**

"Do you know me, oh dear heart? I am but life from the Beloved. Not just mere clay but rather the light of the heart breathed into the heart of dust. I am the soul of the spirit, my heart resides beyond the spheres. My life springs forth from His commanding, Earth from heaven, life hid in dust."[18]

"The wild tulips and the water lilies; the pure and clear current of water; the singing of the birds; the glory of the setting and the rising of the sun and the moon upon the horizon of the sea; the splendor of spring blossoms; the glittering of the dew drops upon the lawn; are but a few of the mani-festations that are the tranquil melodies of the gods hidden behind the veils of nature.

"How ardently I yearn that the arrogance of hearts would be broken once more, that truth would embrace the world, and

souls shine like mirrors, until the dawn when the holy Messengers whispered the psalms of gods upon the face of existence and gave strength to the life of Man!"[19]

IMPORTANT THINGS ABOUT SUFI POETRY

1. Sufi poetry expresses love for God.
2. A "drunken one" is filled with the "wine" of divine love.

CHAPTER 19

Remember This

Remember who you are!
    You are one with God.
    The only sin is forgetting.
    Honor and respect yourself.

Look in your heart!
    Find guidance and truth.
    Your heart does not lie.

Look in your heart to experience God's love;
    Carry that love into the world.

Be filled with compassion, not judgment,
for everyone you meet.
    Let God's love shine through you.

CHAPTER 20

Excerpts from The Gratitude Prayer
By Hazrat Pir Moulana Shah
Maghsoud Sedegh Angha

✲

IN THE NAME OF ALLAH, THE MOST HIGH

AN INFINITE PRAISE, THE ETERNAL salute to the Essence of the One, Allah, the Eternal, the Absolute. He begetteth not, nor is he begotten. He, Who raised the heavens without pillars, spread out the skies and the earth and is firmly established on the Throne. He is the creator of water, lands and trees, the sun and the moon and the cycles of days and nights. He illuminated the heart of Tur Sinai, the horizons of all manifestations and knows the essence of hearts. . . .

Allah, there is no god but He, the Living, the Self-Sustaining, the Eternal, Most Gracious, Most Merciful, Most Majestic, Most Bountiful. . . .

May the heart of the inner travelers be content, continuously. May Islam last eternally. May the sun of the seeker of heart remain illuminated. May the light of the Divine illuminate hearts.[1]

ENDNOTES

INTRODUCTION
1. Abdullah Yusuf Ali, *The Holy Qur'an* (Elmhurst, NY, 1987)

CHAPTER 1: WHAT IS SUFISM?
1. Richard Rohr, *Eager to Love: The Alternative Way of St. Francis of Assisi* (Cincinnati, OH, 2014) *pp. 1-3*

2. Nahid Angha, *The Journey of the Lovers* (San Rafael, CA, 1998) p. 21

3. William C. Chittick, *Sufism: A Beginner's Guide* (Oxford, UK, 2008) p. 119

4. Martin Lings, *What Is Sufism?* (Cambridge, UK, 1993) p. 13

5. Ali Kianfar, *An Introduction to Religion* (San Rafael, CA, 1996) p. 31

6. Nahid Angha, *Principles of Sufism* (San Rafael, CA, 1991) p. 15

7. Nahid Angha, *Lovers*, p. 6

8. Nahid Angha, *Stations of the Sufi Path* (Cambridge, UK, 2010) p. 82

9. Al-Ghazzali, *On Disciplining the Self*, translated by Muhammad Nur Abduls Salam (Chicago, 2010) pp. 29-41

10. Nahid Angha, *Lovers*, p. 9

11. Michael Brill Newman, *The Gift of the Robe* (San Rafael, CA, 2000) quoting Ma'aruf Carchi, p. 24

12. Nahid Angha, *Principles*, p. 74

13. Annemarie Schimmel, *Islam: An Introduction* (Albany, NY, 1992) p. 105

14. Lings, p. 11

15. Seyyed Hossein Nasr, *The Garden of Truth* (New York, 2007) p. 6

16. Ibid., p. 92

17. Ibid., p. 30

18. Lings, p. 127

19. Chittick, p. 19

20. Sarah Hastings Mullin, *The Book of Self* (San Rafael, CA, 2015) p. VII

21. Nahid Angha, *Principles*, pp. 2 & 5

22. Seyyed Hossein Nasr, *The Heart of Islam* (New York, 2002) p. 63

23. Newman, pp. 1-3

24. Nahid Angha, *Principles*, p. 1

25. Stephen Sulyman Schwartz, "How Many Sufis Are There in Islam?" *Huffington Post online*, 9/19/2011

CHAPTER 2: WHAT IS ISLAM?

1. Nasr, *Heart*, pp. 7-8

2. Schimmel, p. 29

3. Nasr, *Heart*, p. 22

4. Frithjof Schuon, *Understanding Islam* (Bloomington, IN, 1994) p. 188

5. *Inspirations on the Holy Qur'an,* from Introduction by Shah Nazar Ali Kianfar, p. 29

6. Mullin, p. 37

7. Nahid Angha, *Lovers,* p. 17

8. Karen Armstrong, *Islam: A Short History* (New York, 2002) p. 5

9. Chittick, p. 6

10. Desmond Stewart, *Mecca* (New York, 1980) p. 17

11. Armstrong, *Islam,* p. 176

12. Arife Ellen Hammerle et al., *Sufi Grace* (Bloomington, IN, 2009) p. 148

13. Nasr, *Heart,* p. 6

14. Hammerle et al., p. 171

15. Nasr, *Heart,* pp. 197-198

16. Hammerle et al., pp. 166-167

17. Dr. Andrew Newberg, "How to Change Your Mind," *The Pennsylvania Gazette* (Philadelphia, PA, May-June, 2016) p. 17

18. Nasr, *Heart,* p. 100

19. Ibid., pp. 15-16

20. Ali Kianfar, *Seasons of the Soul* (San Rafael, CA, 2006) p. 45

21. Mullin, p. 44

22. Nasr, *Heart,* p. 239

23. Chittick, p. 106

24. Lings, p. 13

25. Hammerle et al., p. 189

26. Schuon, p. 33

27. Ibid., p. 156

28. Ibid., p. 33

29. Stewart, p. 11

30. Hammerle et al., p. 159

31. Chittick, p. 7

32. Mullin, p. 33, quoting Ali Kianfar

33. Nasr, *Heart,* p. 6

CHAPTER 3: WHO WAS THE PROPHET MOHAMMAD (PEACE BE UPON HIM)?

1. Karen Armstrong, *Muhammad, A Biography of the Prophet* (New York, 1992), p. 45

2. Mah Talat Etemad-Moghadam Angha, *Al-Momenon: The Faithful,* translated by Nahid Angha (San Rafael, CA, 2000) p. 16

3. Armstrong, *Muhammad,* p. 45

4. Ibid., p. 46

5. Ibid., pp. 48-49

6. M.T.E.M. Angha, p. 23

7. Armstrong, *Islam*, p. 23

8. Armstrong, *Muhammed*, p. 52

9. Houston Smith, *The World's Religions* (New York, 1001) p. 256

Chapter 4: What Is the Holy Qur'an?

1. Schimmel, p. 29

2. Mullin, reporting on Dr. Kianfar's teaching, p. 11

3. Lippman, p. 64

4. Mullin, p. 11

5. *Inspirations*, from an essay by Amelia Amineh Pryor, p. 168

6. *Inspirations,* from Introduction by Dr. Kianfar, p. 39

7. Armstrong, *Islam,* p. 16

8. Andrew Harvey and Anne Baring, *The Divine Feminine* (Berkeley, CA, 1996) p. 120

9. Nasr, *Heart,* p. 25

10. Armstrong, *Islam,* p. 5

11. All quotations are from Abdullah Yusuf Ali, *The Holy Qur'an* (Elmhurst, NY, 1987)

CHAPTER 5: WHAT DOES THE QUR'AN TEACH ABOUT JESUS?

1. Information in this chapter is taken from an article by JoAnn Halima Haymaker "The Prophet Jesus, His Father and Mother," in *Sufism: An Inquiry,* Vol. V, No. 1 (San Rafael, CA, 2010). Unattributed quotations are from the oral teachings of Dr. Ali Kianfar.

2. Nasr, *Heart,* p. 3

3. Kianfar, *Introduction*, quoting Moulana Shah Maghsoud, p. 64

CHAPTER 6: WHAT ARE THE BASIC PRACTICES OF SUFISM?

1. Nahid Angha, *Lovers*, p. 14

2. Nahid Angha, Ibid., p. 14

3. Nahid Angha, *Journey*, p. 17

4. Nahid Angha, Ibid., p. 18

5. Mullin, p. 6

6. Karen Armstrong, *Twelve Steps to a Compassionate Life* (New York, 2010) p. 60

7. Mullin, p. 61

8. Schuon, p. 156

9. Nahid Angha, *Principles*, p. 81

10. Nasr, *Garden*, p. 100

11. Ali Kianfar, *The Zekr* (San Rafael, CA, 1985) p. 19

12. Nahid Angha, *Principles.* p. 82

13. Kianfar, *Zekr,* p. 19

14. Ali Kianfar, *Illumination of the Names* (San Rafael, CA, 2011) p. 12

15. Nahid Angha, *The Nature of Miracle,* (San Rafael, CA, 1993) pp. 15-16

16. Ibid., p. 10

CHAPTER 7: WHAT IS A TEACHER IN SUFISM?

1. Mullin, p. 77

2. Ibid., p. 51

3. Kianfar, *Seasons,* pp. 81-85

CHAPTER 8: WHAT IS THE PURPOSE OF RELIGION?

1. Quoted by Kianfar, *Introduction,* p. 11

CHAPTER 9: WHAT ARE SOME IMPORTANT PRINCIPLES OF SUFISM TAUGHT BY DR. ANGHA AND DR. KIANFAR?

1. Nahid Angha, *Principles*, p. 22

2. Ibid., p. 15

3. Ibid., p. 13

4. Lings, p. 5

5. Nahid Angha, *Principles*, quoting Moulana Shah Maghsoud, p. 23

6. Chittick, p. 43

7. Al Ghazali, p. 8

CHAPTER 10: WHAT ARE THE STEPS ON A SPIRITUAL PATH?

1. Moulana Shah Maghsoud, *Manifestations of Thought*, translated by Nahid Angha (San Rafael, 1980), p. 33

CHAPTER 11: WHAT ARE THE PHYSICAL CULTURE AND THE DIVINE CULTURE?
1. Viktor Frankl, *Man's Search for Meaning* (New York, 1985) pp. 86-87

CHAPTER 13: ARE THERE OTHER QUESTIONS TO BE ANSWERED?
1. Ibn Al 'Arabi, *The Meccan Revelations, Volume I,* translated by William C. Chittick and James W. Morris (New York, 2005) pp. 36-37

2. Ibid., p. 94

3. Amineh Amelia Pryor, in Hammerle, et al. *Sufi Grace* (Bloomington, IN, 2009) p. 117

4. Ibid., p. 122

5. Ibid., p. 122

6. *Inspirations,* from Introduction by Ali Kianfar, p. 15

CHAPTER 14: WHAT IS THE UWAIYSI TARIQAT AND WHO WAS UWAIYS AL QARAN?

1. Nasr, *Garden*, p. 167

2. Newman, p. 36

3. Ibid., p. 71

CHAPTER 17: WHO ARE SOME OTHER SIGNIFICANT MUSLIM AND SUFI WOMEN?

1. Camille Helminski, *Women of Sufism: A Hidden Treasure* (Boston, 2003) p. 5

2. Pryor, in Hammerle, et al., *Sufi Grace*, p. 88

3. M.T.E.M. Angha, p. 37

4. Daniel Ladinsky, *Love Poems from God* (New York, 2002) pp. 1-2

CHAPTER 18: WHAT IS SUFI POETRY?

1. Nahid Angha, *Ecstasy*, pp. 8-9

2. Ibid., p. 16

3. Moulana Shah Maghsoud, *Psalms of God*, translated by Nahid Angha (San Rafael, CA, 1991) pp. 7-8

4. Ladinsky, *Love Poems*, p. 9

5. Nahid Angha, *Ecstasy*, p. 108

6. Ibid., pp. 108-109

7. Coleman Barks, *The Essential Rumi* (Edison, NJ, 1995) from "On Rumi"--unnumbered pages

8. Coleman Barks and Michael Green, *The Illuminated Prayer* (New York, 2000) p. 7

9. Coleman Barks, *The Illuminated Rumi* (New York, 1997) p. 14

10. Ibid., p. 104

11. Ladinsky, *Love Poems*, p. 68

12. Aneela Khalid Arshed, *The Bounty of Allah* (New York, 1999) p. 233

13. Nahid Angha, *Ecstasy*, p. 19

14. Ladinsky, *Love Poems*, p. 150

15. Daniel Ladinsky, *I Heard God Laughing*, (New York, 2006) p. 18

16. Nahid Angha, *Ecstasy*, p. 20

17. Ibid., p. 68

18. Ibid., quoting Moulana Shah Maghsoud, p. 96

19. Moulana Shah Maghsoud, *Psalms*, pp. 11-12

CHAPTER 21: EXCERPTS FROM THE GRATITUDE PRAYER

1. M.T.E.M. Angha, pp. 180-181

GLOSSARY OF TERMS

Adab: inner and outer courtesy, good manners and respect for self and others

Ablution: washing before prayer

Azan: the call to prayer

Eid al-Fitra: Muslim holiday at the end of holy month of Ramadan

Hajj: pilgrimage to Mecca

Hijab: Muslim women's head covering

Jihad: striving to improve oneself

Kaaba (or Kabah): the holy shrine in the center of Mecca that pilgrims circle during the *Hajj*

Khanaghah: meeting place of Sufis

Muezzin: person who recites the call to prayer from the mosque

Ramadan: holy month for Muslims

Sura: chapter in the Qur'an

Tariqat: Sufi order

Zekr: remembrance of God through chanting or repeating holy words or names

BIBLIOGRAPHY

Agnes, Michael, editor, *Webster's New World Dictionary and Thesaurus*, Second Edition (New York, Hungry Minds, Inc.) 2002

Al 'Arabi, Ibn, *The Meccan Revelations, Volume I* (New York, Pir Press) 2005

Al-Ghazzali, *On Disciplining the Self* (Chicago, IL, Great Books of the Islamic World, Inc., 14th Edition) 2010

Ali, Abdullah Yusuf, *The Holy Qur'an* (Elmhurst, NY, Tahrike Tarsile Qur'an, Inc.) 1987

Angha, Hazrat Mir Ghotbeddin Mohammad, *Destination Eternity*, translated by Nahid Angha (San Rafael, CA, International Association of Sufism) 1997

Angha, Mah Talat Etemad-Moghadam, *Al-Momenon: The Faithful*, translated by Nahid Angha (San Rafael, CA, International Association of Sufism) 2000

Angha, Nahid, *Deliverance* (San Rafael, CA, International Association of Sufism) 1995

------, *Ecstasy: The World of Sufi Poetry and Prayer* (San Rafael, CA, International Association of Sufism) 1998

------, *The Journey: Seyr va Soluk* (San Rafael, CA, International Association of Sufism) 1996

------, *The Journey of the Lovers* (San Rafael, CA, International Association of Sufism) 1998

------, *The Nature of Miracle* (San Rafael, CA, International Association of Sufism) 1993

------, *Principles of Sufism* (Fremont, CA, Asian Humanities Press) 1991

------, *Stations of the Sufi Path* (Cambridge, UK, Archetype, 2010)

Angha, Nahid, et al., *Sufi Women: The Journey towards the Beloved* (San Rafael, CA, International Association of Sufism) 1998

Arastu, Salma, *Turning Rumi* (Berkeley, CA, Salma Arastu) 2013

Arshed, Aneela Khalid, *The Bounty of Allah* (New York, The Crossroads Publishing Co.) 1999

Armstrong, Karen, *Islam: A Short History* (New York, Random House) 2002

------, *Muhammad: A Biography of the Prophet* (New York, Harper Collins) 1992

------, *Twelve Steps to a Compassionate Life* (New York, Anchor Books) 2010

Baldick, Julian, *Imaginary Muslims: The Uwaysi Sufis of Central Asia* (New York, New York University Press) 1993

Barks, Coleman, *Delicious Laughter* (Athens, GA, Maypop Books) 1990

------, *The Essential Rumi* (Edison, NJ, Castle Books) 1997

------, *The Illuminated Rumi* (New York, Broadway Books) 1997

------, *The Soul of Rumi* (New York, Harper Collins) 2001

Barks, Coleman and Green, Michael, *The Illuminated Prayer* (New York, Ballantine Books) 2000

Barks, Coleman and Kahn, Inayat, *The Hand of Poetry* (New Lebanon, NY, Omega Publications) 1993

Caravan: Biographies from the Sufism Symposium 1994 – 2014 (San Rafael, CA, International Association of Sufism) 2015

Chittick, William C., *Sufism: A Beginner's Guide* (Oxford, UK, Oneworld Publications) 2008

Ebadi, Shirin, *Iran Awakening* (New York, Random House) 2006

Edson, John Hank, *The Declaration of the Democratic Worldview* (San Francisco, Democracy Press) 2009

------, *Radical Equality* (San Francisco, Democracy Press) 2009

Frankl, Viktor, *Man's Search for Meaning* (New York, Pocket Books) 1985

Hammerle, Arife Ellen, *The Sacred Journey: Unfolding Self Essence* (San Rafael, CA, International Association of Sufism) 2000

Hammerle, Arife Ellen; Newman, Safa Ali Michael; Pryor, Amineh Amelia, *Sufi Grace* (Bloomington, IN, Author House) 2009

Harvey, Andrew, *The Way of Passion: A Celebration of Rumi* (New York, Tarcher/Putnam) 1994

Harvey, Andrew and Anne Baring, *The Divine Feminine* (Berkeley, CA, Conari Press) 1996

Harvey, Andrew and Hanut, Eryk *Perfume of the Desert* (Wheaton, IL, The Theosophical Publishing House) 1999

Haymaker, JoAnn Halima, "Prophet Jesus, His Father and Mother," *Sufism: An Inquiry,*

Vol. XV, No. 1 (San Rafael, CA, International Association of Sufism) Summer 2010

Helminski, Camille, *Women of Sufism: A Hidden Treasure* (Boston, Shambhala Publications) 2003

Helminski, Camille and Helminski, Kabir, *Jewels of Remembrance* (Shambhala Publications, Boston,) 1996

Holy Bible, King James Version (New York, The World Publishing Company) undated

Holy Bible, Revised Standard Version (New York, Thomas Nelson & Sons) 1952

Inspirations on the Holy Qur'an, A Collection of Essays with an introduction by Ali Kianfar (San Rafael, CA, International Association of Sufism) 2013

Kianfar, Shah Nazar Ali, *Illumination of the Names* (San Rafael, CA, International Association of Sufism) 2011

------, *An Introduction to Religion* (San Rafael, CA, International Association of Sufism) 1996

------, *Seasons of the Soul* (San Rafael, CA, International Association of Sufism) 2006

------, *The Zekr* (San Rafael, CA, International Association of Sufism) 1985

Kianfar, Shah Nazar Ali, et al., *Human Self, Volume I: Body* (San Rafael, CA, International Association of Sufism) 2013

Ladinsky, Daniel, *I Heard God Laughing* (New York, Penguin Group (USA), Inc.) 2006

------, *Love Poems from God* (New York, Penguin Group (USA), Inc.) 2002

Levin, E. L., *The Road to Infinity* (San Rafael, CA, International Association of Sufism) 2005

Lings, Martin, *What is Sufism?* (Cambridge, UK, The Islamic Texts Society) 1993

Lippman, Thomas, *Understanding Islam: An Introduction to the Muslim World* (New York, Penguin Books) 1990

Maghsoud, Moulana Shah, *Manifestations of Thought,* translated by Nahid Angha (San Rafael, CA, ETRI Publications) 1980

------, *A Meditation: Payam-e-del*, translated by Nahid Angha (San Rafael, CA, International Association of Sufism) 1994

------, *Psalms of Gods,* translated by Nahid Angha (San Rafael, CA, International Association of Sufism) *1991*

Moore, Daniel Abdal-Hayy, *In the Realm of Neither* (Philadelphia, The Ecstatic Exchange) 2008

Moyne, John and Barks, Coleman, *Open Secret* (Putney, VT, Threshold Books) 1984

Mullin, Sarah Hastings, *The Book of Self* (San Rafael, CA, International Association of Sufism) 2015

Nasr, Seyyed Hossein, *The Garden of Truth: The Vision and Promise of Sufism, Islam's Mystical Tradition* (New York, NY, Harper Collins) 2007

------, *The Heart of Islam: Enduring Values for Humanity* (San Francisco, Harper Collins) 2002

Newberg, Dr. Andrew, "How to Change Your Mind," *The Pennsylvania Gazette* (Philadelphia, University of Pennsylvania) May-June 2016

Newman, Michael Brill, *The Gift of the Robe* (San Rafael, CA, International Association of Sufism) 2000

Ozelsel, Michaela, *Forty Days: A Diary of a Traditional Solitary Sufi Retreat* (Brattleboro, VT, Threshold Books,) 1996

Pryor, Amineh Amelia, *Psychology in Sufism* (San Rafael, CA, International Association of Sufism) 2000

Rohr, Richard, *Eager to Love: The Alternative Way of St. Francis of Assisi* (Cincinnati, OH, Franciscan Media) 2014

Schimmel, Annemarie, *Islam: An Introduction* (Albany, NY, State University of New York) 1992

Schuon, Frithjof, *Understanding Islam* (Bloomington, IN, World Wisdom Books, Inc.) 1994

Schwartz, Stephen Sulyman, "How Many Sufis Are There in Islam?" (Center for Islamic Pluralism, *Huffington Post on-line*) 9/19/2011

Shah, Indris, *The Sufis* (Garden City, NY, Doubleday & Company, Inc.) 1971

Siddiqui, Haroon, *Being Muslim* (Toronto, ON, Canada, Groundwood Books) 2008

Smith, Huston, *The World's Religions* (New York, NY, Harper Collins) 1991

Stewart, Desmond, *Mecca* (New York, Newsweek Books) 1980

Swimme, Brian, .*The Universe is a Green Dragon* (Santa Fe, NM, Bear & Company) 1985

Suhrawardi, Shahabuddin, *The Awarif-ul-Ma'Arif* (Delhi, India, Taj Co.) 2011

Talia, Iman Ali ibn Abu, *Peak of Eloquence* (Elmhurst, NY, Tahrike Tarsile Qur'an, Inc.) 1996

Williamson, Marianne, *Healing the Soul of America* (New York, Touchstone) 2000

ACKNOWLEDGEMENTS

I WISH TO EXPRESS MY gratitude to Dr. Nahid Angha and Dr. Ali Kianfar for their guidance in this project and for much of my life. Thanks also to Sheikh Jamal Granick and Judith Dehnert for careful reading of drafts of this book and to Katie Watts for professional proof-reading. My appreciation goes to Amineh Amelia Pryor and Hamid John Hank Edson for their help and advice from their publishing experience. Thank you also to Matthew Davis, Ph.D., of BEAR INTERNATIONAL PremiereGraphicDesignInstitute, for the cover design.